DEBBIE POTTER

EBONY
&
IVORY

PROMOTING PEACE, LOVE, AND UNITY IN A RACIST WORLD

ISBN: 979-8-9931247-0-4

References and Disclaimer

References

All Scripture quotations are from the New Century Version unless otherwise noted by initials, and all emphasis is mine unless otherwise noted.

Scripture quotations from The Holy Bible, New Century Version, Copyright 2005 by Thomas Nelson, Inc. Used by Permission.

Scripture taken from the Holy Bible, New International Version, Copyright 1973, 1978, 1984 by International Bible Society. Used by permission of Zondervan Publishing House. As this is not my primary source, these will be identified with the initials NIV.

Disclaimer

In all the true stories used as examples, all names (except Dewey's, my own, and some family members) and some places have been changed to respect the privacy of others.

Dedication

I first want to dedicate this book to my Father God, His Son Jesus Christ, and His Holy Spirit Who dwells within me. Without God and His Word, I would have nothing to share.

Secondly, I want to dedicate this book to the memory of my late husband Dewey, whom God used in such a powerful way to share His Love to me and so many others. I finished the first draft of this book on what would have been his sixty-fourth birthday.

Acknowledgments

I would like to thank and acknowledge Steve Harrison's "Get Published Now" staff, especially Sarah Brown, who gave me some individual coaching sessions and encouraged me along the way.

I also want to thank all my family and friends who supported me during this journey. Thank you to my wonderful first readers for all your valuable comments. Thank you, Tami Whitmore and Cassie Valler, for giving me advice and showing me the self-publishing ropes in person.

Thank you, Pam Kindle, for being so patient with me and editing my book to make it more readable and still share the message God has placed on my heart. Your time, consideration, and encouragement have been priceless.

Thanks most of all to my Heavenly Father, who made all of this possible and who gives me life, love, peace, joy, and hope forevermore.

Introduction

Have you ever had a vision? I mean a real-life message that seemed to be delivered straight from God? I have had that experience only once in my life; this book addresses one of the major problems in our world that He brought to my attention through that experience, along with the surprising solution.

Do you ever get disgusted or discouraged – or maybe downright terrified of the confusion and chaos caused by racism? Do you wonder if it is even possible for you to make a difference – to *be* the change? If so, Ebony & Ivory: Promoting Peace, Love, and Unity in a Racist World is for you! It reveals how you are being manipulated by the media and the masses to be racist, but it doesn't leave you there. Instead, it gives you the tools you need to get back your God-given rights – no matter your skin color, nationality, socio-economic status, or even your past.

You can't live in this world without being bombarded with racism and prejudice. You may even be living in the midst of a crippled city that has been ravaged by riots and hatred. Racism is a deadly disease sent from the devil, who disguises himself in various ways.

I had heard rumors of what the inner city of Portland, Oregon looked like, but nothing could have prepared me for the devastation and filth that attacked my senses in October of 2022 as I exited the freeway onto a street advertising fuel and food on the outskirts of town. Dirty tents lined one edge of the road with various pieces of clothing and trash littering the small areas between. The other side of the road held a variety of businesses: gas stations, fast-food establishments, chain department stores, grocery stores, etc. I really needed fuel *and* a restroom, but the first three service stations I saw all had signs out front saying "No Restrooms." The stench from across the street filled my nostrils. I was desperate; I finally went in search of a fast food establishment where I could purchase something just so I could use the restroom. *Then* I went back to get fuel.

What had happened to the beautiful city I had grown to love back when I was attending a small Christian college in 1980? Areas similar to this one used to have roadsides filled with green grass, shrubs, and beautiful flowers; but now instead there was dirt, trash, and hovels. Back then, even Skid Row didn't look this bad! My college missions class had spent every Saturday morning at a local Gospel Mission sharing the gospel message and breakfast with the street people who had attended. In all that time, I never once felt afraid or repelled, as I was when I drove through the outskirts of Portland that early fall morning in 2022. The street people I'd seen and spent time with in 1980 were grateful for a warm meal and fellowship, and they had been presented *hope* from the gospel; whereas the scene before me in 2022 reflected disrespect and disregard for the personage and property of others, and the few faces I'd seen at that hour in the morning reflected hopelessness and despair.

I wondered what made the difference. Was it just the passage of time? I knew that wasn't it because I'd driven in and around other big cities that didn't have this ugliness on display for all the world to see. So what was the difference? Towards the end of that month-long trip in 2022, I was able to visit a friend named Tommy who had been a mere teen when my husband had been a minister in Eastern Washington. Tommy had moved with his family to the Portland area while he was still a young teen; but as an adult, he had become an officer in the military as well as a police officer in Portland. From him, I learned that this street in Portland displayed only a small segment of a much bigger problem, a problem caused by hatred and prejudice and fed by the media and the masses who had been manipulated to believe a lie.

According to Tommy, when he first returned from a mission overseas to his job as a police officer in Portland in the spring of 2020, the media was showing clips of what appeared to be a horrible act of violence against a black man by the name of George Floyd. Whether this act was intentional and motivated by prejudice on the part of these officers as it *appeared* to be or whether (as Tommy suspected) the video was edited by the media to only allow the public to see what they *wanted* us to see, we were led to believe that *all* police officers were murderers and were "out to get" *all* black people.

My husband Dewey frequently counseled people during his thirty-plus years in the ministry; he wisely advised, "When communicating, especially in areas of disagreement or differences of opinion, avoid using or listening to words like *all, everyone, always* and *never.*"

In recent years, terms like "wokeness" and "Critical Race Theory" have come to represent something completely different than their original definitions. At first, people were encouraged to "be aware" of the needs of others and monitor attitudes and laws to make sure they were fair to everyone. Now the media would like you to believe that *all* white people (or *all* of any particular race, color or profession) are considered *inherently* evil and prejudiced. This is simply not true; and I, for one, don't like being lied to! Jesus called the devil "the father of lies" and "a liar from the beginning"; so ultimately, *satan* is the one behind all the lies and evil that cause hate and discontent in this world.

According to Tommy, this is what really happened: In 2020, after the public had been bombarded with propaganda promoting prejudice, some extremist groups calling themselves "Black Lives Matter" (BLM) and "Antifa" (a contraction of the phrase, anti-fascist) infiltrated the city of Portland and instigated riots with the use of mob mentality. (You know that ALL lives matter, but this first group was able to use their name to hide their *true* agenda.)

Using the cover of darkness during these 2020 riots, this group and those who blindly followed them did unspeakable things to all kinds of innocent people. They claimed to be standing up for their rights, but they were actually breaking all kinds of laws themselves and taking away the rights of those who had lived and worked there for years. These rioters broke into businesses by throwing rocks and other heavy objects through windows. They pillaged and plundered and sometimes destroyed by fire. Many business owners of varying ethnicities tried to rebuild, only to have their businesses destroyed again; so they were forced to close down and sometimes even to move away.

Tommy said people in power refused to acknowledge that these things were really a problem; so the rights of *life* and *liberty* were taken away from the locals, while the *rights* of the rioters were being protected. Now the lives and welfare of the law-abiding citizens were in jeopardy, and those in the police force who had sworn "to serve and protect" were not allowed the authority to do their job. In fact, the rioters who had yelled obscenities at the police and displayed nasty signs all along, now turned their efforts on the police headquarters and courthouse and upped their game. These groups threw rocks, bottles, and other dangerous objects at them; and yet those public servants weren't allowed to defend themselves or government property. What's wrong with this picture?!! Isn't it interesting that most of the media avoided showing *those* videos?

Don't get me wrong. I am *not* suggesting that *all* media is bad or that it is *solely* responsible for spreading racism and prejudice, as will be evidenced in the next story I will share. I *will* say that sifting through the news is harder than it used to be, so we need to be alert.

I was extremely naive in my early twenties when I moved to Seattle to live and work. I lived with a few Christian girls, and they helped me learn how to navigate the big city. I had not dated at all in the little town I grew up in, so I accepted dates with almost every guy who asked me out. Many of these guys were of different races, and some were even from other countries (including, but not limited to, Nigeria, Ethiopia, Mexico, the Czech Republic, Iraq, and Iran). I met many of these guys through my roommates, in our apartment building, or at church functions; so I felt pretty safe. Through them, I was introduced to a variety of lifestyles and traditions. The guy in the story I am about to share with you was an acquaintance of a friend from church. For the sake of anonymity, I'll call him Joe and our mutual friend John.

As I was visiting friends after the worship service, I noticed that John had a visitor with him who didn't seem to know many people; so I went over to introduce myself and make him feel welcomed. John introduced me to Joe (a very attractive young black man), and we talked for several minutes. He seemed very nice; so when he asked me if I'd be interested in going out, I told him I would love to. He lived in a downtown apartment, while I lived and worked in the north end. Like many people who lived and worked downtown, Joe didn't own a car; so we agreed to meet at a restaurant downtown, and I planned to drive him home after our date.

Joe and I enjoyed a nice dinner at an upscale restaurant in downtown Seattle. Our dinner conversation had been light and pleasant, and I felt like things were going pretty well. Maybe we would go out again. Joe was easy to talk to, and he seemed genuinely interested in me.

After our meal, Joe directed me to his apartment building. I carefully negotiated Seattle traffic as we discussed what sports we enjoyed watching or being involved in when we had spare time. After pulling into the three-story apartment's large parking lot, I turned off the car, and we concluded the conversation we had begun after leaving the restaurant.

For the first time that evening, I felt a little awkward. I had never driven a date to his home before, so I wasn't sure how to say goodnight without being rude and telling him the date was over. Nor did I feel comfortable offering to walk him to his door. After a moment of silence, Joe asked if I wanted to come up to his apartment. I politely declined, saying that I really should get home before too late.

I had grown up in a home where we didn't have friends of the opposite sex in our bedrooms or anywhere that wasn't out in the open or in public, so I truly expected Joe to get out of the car and politely say goodnight or even ask if I wanted to go out again. Instead, he looked at me with an expression that showed what he thought and then he put it into words...

"It's because I'm black, isn't it? You're afraid to come up to my apartment because I'm black?"

"Of course not!" I answered. (The thought had never even occurred to me.)

"If you're not prejudiced, then you'll come up. If you are... I get it."

Call me naive or just stupid, but now I felt I had to *prove* that I wasn't prejudiced; so I tentatively followed him up to his apartment, telling him I couldn't stay long. His apartment was nice and clean; but I got nervous when he dimmed the lighting, put on some soft, romantic music and asked if I'd like something to drink. I told him I'd take some ice water, and he walked into the kitchen to get our drinks. Now what was I going to do?! I started to panic, thinking of hundreds of scenarios I *should have* considered *before* coming up to his third floor apartment!

As my pulse raced in fear, I blurted out, "I just want you to know that I am a virgin and intend to stay that way until I'm married." *That* certainly got his attention.

He jumped back into the front room like he'd been snake-bitten, "You what?!"

I repeated the statement, blushing due to the sensitivity of the subject.

He responded with a wary, "No way," as he shook his head slowly. "How old are you?"

"Yes way," I countered, "and I'm twenty-two. I'm not weird or anything, but remaining a virgin is a *decision* I made because of my belief in following God's ways. I am tempted just like any other young lady, but God has always given me strength and a way out of compromising situations."

At first, he seemed a little relieved that he hadn't tried to seduce a minor; but then he just stood there with an incredulous look on his face, our two drinks still in his hands.

I used that opportunity to let myself out of the apartment and forced myself to calmly walk to my car instead of running frantically the way I was tempted to. Again, all kinds of scenarios ran through my head. How could I have fallen for the line Joe had used? I cannot judge this young man's motives – maybe he really believed I was afraid of him because he was black; but I *felt* that I had been manipulated by him to believe I had to *prove* I wasn't racist. I berated myself all the way home. I knew my roommates would want to know how my date went, and I dreaded having to relive the whole humiliating event.

Even now as I look back on my naivety, I am embarrassed; but I am also thankful that God protected me in my predicament and provided a way out, as He has promised in Scripture (I Corinthians 10:11-13). I now call the tactic Joe seemed to use *reverse racism,* but it's still racism. I hope that my sharing can help other young people avoid this kind of situation altogether. Never let someone, whether using racism or moral compromise, convince you that you have to *prove* your feelings or beliefs by putting yourself in uncomfortable or compromising circumstances. I am not calling Joe a bully or a predator. Years later, however, I learned that bullies and predators are *also* known to try to convince their prey to feel stupid or to even believe that *they* are the ones in the wrong - leaving victims afraid to speak out and feeling isolated. If you or someone you know is currently in such a situation, realize that you are not alone. Confide in a trusted friend or relative who can help you get the support you need. You might be surprised to find how common your experiences may be and how many help groups are available.

You may not live in a big city like Portland, Oregon, where the 2020 racial riots occurred or in Seattle, Washington, where I lived as a naive young woman; so you may wonder what this subject has to do with you. In Ebony & Ivory: Promoting Peace, Love, and Unity in a Racist World, you will learn how this problem of racism and prejudice affects you and what you can do about it. You will learn that if you claim to be a Christian, you are called not only to *love* your neighbors and enemies, but also to love "*as Christ first loved you*." God does not judge you by your race, color, or even political affiliation. Instead, He offers you the free gifts of mercy, grace, and love (even though you don't *deserve* them); and He calls you to share those same gifts with everyone else – without prejudice.

I have had the privilege of reading through the Bible several times in my life and have learned, through my studies, to appreciate the wealth of profound wisdom provided in God's Word. I rely heavily on this wisdom in my life *and* in this book. I also rely on a special dream story inspired by the principles taught in the Biblical book of Ephesians (which I share in chapter 1). My own life experiences (both good and bad) - as a daughter, preacher's wife, mother, widow, friend, teacher, and child of God - as well as the teachings and life experiences of others are also used to take you on a journey *out* of this world of darkness, destruction, and death and *into* the world of light, love, and life.

By reading and applying the principles in this book, you will find the treasures you need to have peace, love, and harmony in your own life and find out how *you* can *change the world* for the better through the power of God's Spirit.

You will discover:

- How having a relationship with God is the cornerstone to overcoming racism

- That God wants to adopt YOU, no matter your race, color, social status, past, etc.

- How YOU can use YOUR unique gifts to combat racism and impact millions of lives

...and so much more. Join me in *my dream* for Peace, Love, and Unity!

Contents

Chapter 1

Can This Dream Come True? My Dream Story

WHAM! Gram Tilly woke with a start at the sound of a door slamming down the hall, followed by the thunderous roar of her great-grandchildren's feet racing towards her as she sat in her favorite rocking chair in their living room. She raised a shaking hand to steady her fluttering heart.

Now twelve-year-old Tina was yelling at her eight-year-old brother Tim, "You stupid brat!"

"I know you are, but what am I?" he retorted.

Gram wondered what had happened to cause all this ruckus. She must have dozed off while the kids had been playing a board game in the other room and their mom (her granddaughter Lydia) was busy preparing tonight's Christmas Eve dinner. Earlier today Gram and the kids had made Christmas cookies to give to friends and neighbors, and they'd cut out dozens of paper snowflakes to decorate their windows - but they'd evacuated the kitchen when their mom had come in to begin dinner preparations. At that time, everyone had seemed happy enough.

Gram was a feisty eighty-year-old with a mischievous glint in her eye and a spring in her step. She loved God and children more than anything else in the world, and they all loved her right back. This past week must have caught up with her a bit for her to have nodded off like that. The last thing she remembered was reflecting on this past year; she could hardly believe 1955 was almost over. She remembered feeling the warmth and peace flowing through her veins as she had watched the colorful flames licking up the wood in the fireplace. The gentle crackling and popping of the fire mingled with the harmonious sound of Lydia's voice as she sang while preparing their meal had seemed to drown out the howling of the wind outside and allowed her to truly enjoy the beauty of the pure driven snow without dwelling on the bitter cold. And the smells – ahhh, the tantalizing smells of cedar smoke, of roasting turkey and dressing, and the delicious and comforting smells of sweet and spicy vanilla, nutmeg, ginger, and cloves. No wonder she'd slipped into such a sweet slumber!

The first several days of vacation had been filled with loads of fun outdoor activities. Gram had joined the neighborhood kids in ice skating on the frozen pond at the Smith's house down the road. She'd helped them build snowmen and forts and had even joined in on their snowball fights. Gram had watched the kids longingly as they'd traipsed, with their sleds, up the hill at the park to ride down over and over again till they could climb no more. She was in pretty good shape, but she couldn't risk breaking any bones at this age, so she just enjoyed watching all the kids have fun.

All the moms on the block had been cooking, cleaning, and preparing for the holidays. Still, they always seemed to know just when the kids would all come in with shiny red cheeks and noses and freezing fingers and toes; so they would have soothing hot chocolate and cookies ready and waiting. When the dads got off work, the kids would all be washed up and ready for dinner.

The kids had been enjoying their freedom from schoolwork, and Gram Tilly had been thoroughly enjoying her holiday with the kids; but all outdoor activities had come to a screeching halt a few days ago when a record-breaking storm had come in. It had chased everyone indoors, and now nobody went outside unless it was absolutely necessary. Lydia and Gram had tried to keep Tim and Tina occupied with fun games and activities; but as demonstrated by her earlier outburst, even mild-mannered Tina seemed to be at a breaking point - and being stuck inside was definitely not Tim's cup of tea. Everyone's nerves seemed to be shot, and Gram felt a tiny sigh escape as she contemplated sharing her special story about the true meaning of Christmas with them. She looked at the grumpy faces of the children and knew that it was definitely time; so she called them to her.

"I know you two would probably rather watch the new television or listen to a radio program, but could you humor an old woman and listen to a story?" she cajoled.

Tina uncharacteristically rolled her eyes and let out an exaggerated sigh, "I suppose – if it's not *too* long."

"Or too *boring!*" Tim mumbled, scowling at the world.

Gram chuckled, saying, "I'll do my very best...."

⪻⬥⪼

"Long ago, in the days of the horse and buggy, there was a little girl who was just about your age, Tina; and she had a little brother, too. Her name was Margaret, Maggie for short; and his name was Stephen, but she always called him *Stevie* unless he made her angry. This was one of those days that she couldn't *stand* Stephen, and just looking at him got her blood boiling. She'd had a cough and sore throat for about a week, and it hurt so bad that it even woke her up at night. The pain and lack of sleep were making her irritable; so when Stephen tapped her shoulder for the third time in the last two minutes, she burst out in a rage.

'Why can't you just leave me alone, Stephen? Can't you see that I'm sick?!'

As Maggie began coughing uncontrollably, five-year-old Stevie hung his head to hide his tears and mumbled as he quietly laid down his slate, 'I just wanted to show you the picture I drew.'

Before Maggie could even respond, there was a stomping sound outside the big wooden door, followed by a gust of icy wind and blowing snow as Papa appeared inside, pushing the door closed with one hand as he removed his hat with the other. His cheeks were bright and red from the cold, but his eyes sparkled. He had so much to be thankful for this holiday season, including his warm coat, hat and gloves – but most of all, his family.

'Children!' Papa exclaimed, 'I have something very special for all of us this Christmas Eve. I met an old man traveling through town today, and he insisted we have these gifts. Stevie, why don't you go get Mama from the kitchen? I want all of us to be together when I open these.'

Stevie pulled a reluctant Mama from the kitchen. She had a scowl on her face, flour on her nose, and fresh bread dough stuck to her fingers. As she held up her hands towards Papa's startled face, she asked in a frustrated tone, 'Can't you see that I'm in the middle of kneading bread? I've been working all day to prepare this special dinner, and I'm not about to let you ruin it now!'

As Mama spoke, the children spotted a little wood chip falling from something in Papa's pocket.

'Papa!' they chorused as they both pushed toward the pocket that held their hidden treasures.

'Oh no you don't!' Papa responded, chuckling as he drew them both into his lap. His tone sobered as he continued, 'These are special presents that you must be ready to receive. The man who gave them to us warned that they would only be beautiful if the people who received them were kind to each other. Each person is to use their special talents to serve and build one another up in love. The old man even *prayed* that we would be ready to receive his gifts.'

When Papa finished speaking, he pulled three small gifts from his pocket. Each one was an intricately carved and beautifully painted wooden ornament that was to be placed on the Christmas tree. Papa handed one to each child and one to Mama, and then he pulled out his own. Each ornament had a few words on it, and when placed together, they read: *Peace on Earth, Goodwill Toward Men.*

The smile Mama usually wore had returned to her face until she saw that a tiny chip of wood was missing from her gift. 'What happened to *my* ornament?' she asked in a dejected tone.

Papa reached over, rubbing his large finger across the rough spot where the chip was missing. 'Ah, it's nothing a little sandpaper can't fix,' he assured her as he bundled his coat a little tighter and headed back out to the shed where he kept a small supply of sandpaper with other wood-working tools.

'Maggie, Stevie, start getting cleaned up for dinner. It'll be ready shortly.'

Mama had barely finished her request and returned to the kitchen when Stevie turned towards Maggie, made a disgusting face, and stuck out his tongue. Trying to ignore her ill-mannered brother was going to be more difficult than usual this evening, so Maggie turned her attention to the newly hung ornaments. Almost immediately, she noticed something unusual about her brother's ornament. *His* was now missing a piece, just like Mama's!

'You stupid brat, how'd you chip your ornament already?' Maggie sneered at her brother; but as she turned to show the flaw to him, she stopped dead in her tracks as she witnessed another piece fall – this time from her *own* ornament.

A cold gust of snow swirled around Papa as he turned to firmly close the door. After removing his coat and hat, he turned to see Maggie and Stevie, both with guilty looks on their faces. He crossed the room in two great strides and yelled, 'What did y'all do to your gifts? I was only gone for a few minutes and you've already ruined them!' But as the words left his mouth, he noticed a tiny flake of wood come drifting down from his own ornament without anyone touching it.

Bewildered, he sat down and began sanding Mama's ornament. This was obviously going to take some time. Had the old man given him gifts that were worthless and were just going to fall apart? Maggie and Stevie just stood looking between the ornaments, each other, and Papa, trying to comprehend what was happening.

Mama came in to announce that dinner was ready, but she came to an abrupt halt when she saw the looks on their faces. She jokingly asked, 'What's with all these looks you're giving me? Don't you know that I love y'all more than life and wouldn't make you eat something that would poison you?'

The children laughed a little, and a big smile appeared on Papa's lips. Just as he started to say something kind in return, Mama smiled and exclaimed, 'I thought you just got back from the shed! How'd you fix my gift so quickly?'

'Oh, I'm far from finished,' he replied; but when he looked down, he realized that Mama's ornament *had* returned to its original beauty. Papa continued in a dazed voice, excitement building as realization dawned. 'It seems like these decorations really *are* something special! Remember what I told you the old man said about how we should treat each other? It seems that if we're saying, doing, or even thinking things from a good heart, the ornaments are beautiful beyond compare; but if we get mean, ugly, and hateful, they get ugly too. I guess I didn't really believe the old man.'

'But it does seem to be true,' Mama responded; 'so let's be thankful and learn our lessons.' She put a hand on each of the children's heads and said, 'Do you know how awful you've acted towards each other all day? If your father had gotten these things this morning, they'd be nothin' but sawdust by now.'

At first both children hung their heads in shame, but then Maggie looked at Stephen and thought about how this was all *his* fault. She allowed her mind to dwell on all the irritating things he'd said and done, and how annoyed she'd been with him. The next thing she knew, she was thinking of all kinds of ways she could get back at him for making her miserable; but when she saw her ornament suddenly *covered* with little holes cut out by her own mean thoughts, she was crushed and began to sob uncontrollably.

Papa put his arms around her, and Mama smoothed back her long hair. Stevie even came over to stand by her; but his concerned eyes just made her cry harder because deep down in her heart she knew that he really did love her, and this really wasn't his fault.

Mama turned to face Maggie and asked in a gentle voice, 'Would you like for us to help you learn how to love your brother *all* the time, even when you're sick or hurt or angry?'

Maggie smiled up at Mama through her tears, 'You know I would, Mama.'

Then Mama turned a loving but stern face toward her son. 'Stevie, you're going to have to try just as hard as she does. It isn't just about not being mean, but also about using your time to help your sister and by saying nice things to her.'

Stevie met the challenge with his eyes and exclaimed, 'Yes, Ma'am. I'll do my very bestest!'

Mama smiled at the children and then looked up at her husband. As the adults' eyes met, they knew their own lessons were about to begin, as well. Long and hard lessons they would be – both to learn and to teach.

That evening as they ate the delicious meal Mama had worked so hard to prepare, they practiced showing their love for each other by being kind in the things they said as they shared their day. Papa worked hard every day at the blacksmith's shop in town to provide for his family. Mama made their home such a warm and cozy place with her love, hard work, and sense of humor. Each day, the children would do their chores; and then Mama would teach them their lessons at the kitchen table. Since they didn't have a school in town yet, Mama did her best to teach them to read and write and do their sums while Papa was at work.

Maggie tried especially hard to say encouraging things to her family tonight, even though talking sent searing pain down her throat and caused her to cough. She knew she had a special gift of bringing out the best in others; even though it hurt to talk, she really wanted to please God.

In view of all they'd learned so far, Papa and Stevie went out of their way to help clear the table and wash the dishes - something they would never even have thought of before. When everything was put away, Papa pulled out the big family Bible; after leading them in prayer, he began to read from the book of Ephesians once more. The preacher had challenged the church to read the book of Ephesians every day for one week. After Papa read tonight, he asked everyone to share their favorite part.

'I'll begin,' Papa said in his deep bass voice. 'I'm glad that this book shares the great mystery – that God broke down the barriers between the Jews and the Gentiles through the blood of Jesus so we could all be one in Christ and be built together into a holy temple for Him.'

Mama shared that she liked the part about being thankful and singing, making melody in your hearts to the Lord. Everyone smiled, knowing how much she loved to sing all day long as she did her chores.

Maggie said she was glad that she could be forgiven because of the blood of Jesus and that His Spirit would help her put away her anger and instead be kind, loving, and forgiving. She also liked how everyone was given certain gifts to bless the others.

Stevie was so excited to share his favorite. With boyish enthusiasm, he brandished a pretend sword and shield and told how he would beat the evil one. The rest of the family laughed, realizing that the sword and shield spoken of in Ephesians were actually the armor of God's Word and faith.

As they settled back into a reflecting mode, they heard a timid knock at the door. They exchanged puzzled looks as Papa got up, muttering, 'Now, who in their right minds would be out on such a cold night?'

When Papa opened the door, the whole family just stared in shock at the sight of six cold and hungry dark-skinned faces. Even though they lived fairly close to Fort Laramie in Wyoming, Maggie and Stevie rarely got to go down to town – and never had gone inside the fort; so neither of them had ever seen a black person before. They knew that Mama and Papa were against the idea of slavery, and they were all glad the Civil War had ended years ago; but now, here they were face to face with people that many of their family, friends, and neighbors might still refer to as *heathens*.

The large man before them spoke in a humble manner, 'My name is Joshua; this is my wife Sarah, our sons Jonathan and David, and our daughters Mary and Elizabeth. When our buggy broke down today just out of town on our way out West, we tried to find a place to stay for the night; but the people at the inn said they were full. We'd almost given up hope when we met a fellow Christian who gave us these ornaments and said you might be able to give us a warm place to stay tonight?'

Papa's mind was racing. He had smiled at all the Bible names in this new family, but he didn't know them from Adam. He had just read about Jesus coming to break down the walls of hatred between the Jews and the Gentiles, making them into one body for the Lord. Could this principle apply to blacks and whites as well? He knew he'd be taking a tremendous risk with the social standing of his entire family if he allowed these people to stay - but what would Jesus want him to do? He thought about how the book of Ephesians was all about the love of Christ, the unity of His church, and how Christians should live. Then, without further hesitation, he smiled and firmly grasped Joshua's hand in welcome.

'Please come in out of this dreadful cold. My name is Joseph; this is my wife Ruth, our daughter Margaret, and our son Stephen. We would love for you to stay and spend Christmas with us.'

Mama and Maggie immediately began warming dinner for this new family as Papa and Stevie hung their coats. Papa brought two extra chairs from the living room so Joshua's family could all sit at the table, while his own family stood around the kitchen. Soon both families were laughing and talking as if they'd known one another for years; but as they all moved toward the front room, they were startled to hear a firm knock at the door. Knowing the prejudices in this small town, Papa cautiously opened the door, unconsciously shielding Joshua with his own body.

Papa, Mama, Maggie, and Stevie watched with jaws dropped as their *entire* church family, young and old, filed into their house, each holding ornaments similar to the ones they'd all received. Everyone was being careful to say only good and encouraging things (although seeing a black family in their midst was quite a shock and normally would have caused a considerable stir had it not been for the lessons they'd all been learning from the ornaments).

When all were crowded into the house and the door had been closed, Papa turned to the two nearest men. 'Hello, Jim. How are you doing, Mark? It seems like we've all been running into the same old man,' he said with a smile.

Jim grinned at Papa as he and Mark held up nearly identical wooden ornaments, 'These seem to be pretty plentiful, but I wouldn't give up mine for a whole pocketful of gold.'

'No, I don't think any of us would either,' Papa said, thinking of all they'd gained in just one evening, 'but why is everyone coming here?'

'Didn't he tell you? The old man told us we should all meet together at your house and that we would be incredibly blessed,' Jim answered.

Just then there was *another* knock. Once more, Papa opened the door, this time to the stranger who had bestowed all these wonderful gifts upon them. Quietly, this old gentleman led everyone to hang their ornaments on the tree. When the last one was hung, an expectant hush filled the crowded room. Suddenly, each of the individual ornaments joined together to become one inspiring masterpiece that glowed and warmed as if suddenly filled with light; and then they began to issue forth the most beautiful sound of praise to God, singing, *Peace on Earth, Goodwill to Men.* Soon, everyone in the house joined together in perfect harmony.

The remaining people in their little town heard the joyful sound and saw the heavenly glow; it was as if the whole world knew that those in the little house on the hill were Jesus' disciples because of the love they had for one another.

The old stranger was the last to leave; as Papa and Joshua stood watching him walk away, they saw the man's hair turning almost white - then his figure seemed to fade away until he simply wasn't there. They wondered if they had, as the Scriptures taught, *entertained angels unawares*."

It took a few minutes for Gram to return to reality. She looked down at Tina and Tim, who had unexpectedly listened to the whole story without a peep. "Do you understand now why it is so important to love each other from a pure heart, even when you don't feel like it?"

"Sort of," Tina said reluctantly, "but that wasn't *real;* it was just a story." Her tone of voice caught Gram by surprise, but before she could even respond, the children's dad walked in the door.

"Tim! Tina! Honey! Come look at what I have for you! An old man traveling through town gave us these special ornaments...." He stopped short as he saw Tim and Tina looking at his wife's grandmother as if she'd just come back from the dead. "Maggie.... What did you tell these kids that's got them all spooked? They look like they've just seen a ghost."

Maggie simply smiled as the children's mother came out of the kitchen with a scowl on her face, flour on her nose, and fresh bread dough stuck to her fingers....

That is *my dream,* the dream God gave me back in 1996 when Dewey had encouraged our congregation to read Ephesians each day for a week, back when our children were little. In fact, in the dream, it was my own family and I who received the ornaments that Dewey had brought home from a stranger; and I was the one who had such a sore throat and cough (that part was reality and what woke me up). Most of my dreams had been very disjointed and didn't make much sense, even if I could remember details; but this dream was so vivid that I had to get up and type all the details I could remember. I felt an instant call to share this dream with others. After I shared it with my family, my brother Andy asked if he could prayerfully change it from dream form into story form. I gladly accepted his offer; although he changed the characters and added a little to the story line - and I've made several revisions over the years - the *principles* all come from God's Word and, therefore, are *unchangeable* (Hebrews 4:12; II Peter 1:20-21; James 1:16-18).

I believe with all my heart that God has the power to change hearts and lives, and He graciously allows us to be involved in His work (Matthew 9:37-38; II Corinthians 6:1; Philippians 1:4-6). YOU can use YOUR gifts to build up and encourage others in love just as Maggie and her family were able to do in this dream story (which I will address more fully in chapter 9). In the chapters to follow, we will discuss where racism comes from and what we can do about it outside of the political arena.

Chapter 2

Where Does Racism Come From?

The year was 1966. The late June air was dry, hot, and oppressive in this small farming town in Eastern Washington. Standing in line about halfway up was twenty-one-year-old Betty, who was fairly sure that neither this line nor her last month of pregnancy were *ever* going to come to an end. This pretty young brunette was small in stature but not in heart, as was evidenced in her sparkling blue eyes. Her studious four-year-old daughter clung to her left hand, scanning the room with inquisitive green eyes, slightly damp honey-colored hair curled lightly down to her shoulders. Betty was thankful that her normally active two-year-old son was tucked safely against her shoulder and atop her protruding belly as he slept peacefully amidst the buzzing of English and Spanish conversations around them.

Betty was trying to be patient, but moisture beaded on her forehead and mixed with the dust from their 5-mile trip into town in the old farm truck. As a result, she felt sweaty, swollen, dirty, grimy, and exhausted. The school clock on the cafeteria wall showed she'd only been waiting twenty minutes, but to her mind and body, it felt like hours. Someone had opened the windows trying to cool the air; but with no breeze, it did little to alleviate her discomfort. Though the trees outside gave the illusion of shade, they did nothing to ease the stifling heat indoors as the sun beat down unmercifully. She did feel a *little* comforted by the slightly fresher air and enjoyed watching the birds as they flitted from tree to tree and listening to their harmonious songs.

To further distract herself from the heat and her swollen body, she looked around at the other ladies standing in line. They were all lower/middle class women, mostly white, stay-at-home moms. Most, like her, probably had husbands who were at their jobs. Although probably half the women in town were Hispanic, about seventy-five percent of today's group were Caucasian; most of the Mexican women were out in the fields or orchards working alongside their husbands and children. Betty figured she would be the youngest adult in the room; in fact, most of these ladies were probably in their late twenties to early thirties and had school-aged children. Still, since it was a small town, she was a little surprised she didn't recognize anyone close to her in line.

Suddenly, young Debra let go of her hand and tugged her maternity top, pointing a little finger at the lone black woman about a yard ahead of them. Betty cringed as she heard her little girl's *loud* exaggerated whisper filled with awe, "Mommy, Mommy, look! That lady is chocolate!"

Betty immediately tried to shush Debra and at the same time turned a hundred shades of red. Her heart beat erratically as she slowly raised her eyes full of terror and apology to meet those of the black woman who by now, of course, had turned to face them. You could have heard a pin drop as everyone in the room waited with baited breath to see how this rather large black woman would respond. Would she become indignant or violent? If she did, this young pregnant mom wouldn't stand a chance! The tension was palpable; but when this friendly black woman's face split into a huge smile - first aimed at the obviously excited little girl who had just encountered the first black person she'd ever seen and then at the girl's terrified mother - one could hear the collective sigh of relief.

⸻◆⸻

I was that little girl. Surprisingly enough, I don't remember this incident; but I heard my mother tell it several times while I was growing up when *embarrassing moments* came up in conversation. I truly believe this gracious woman is probably largely responsible for my lack of prejudice and my zeal for justice and equality for all. Had this woman responded in anger or violence, I probably would have been scarred for life and had a very different view. What did it cost her? She seemed to understand the innocence of a child. She made the choice to be humble and gracious and to look for the good in others, rather than to buy into the lie that all white people looked down on her and hated her because of the color of her skin. She chose truth.

At that time in my life, we lived about five miles out of town and didn't have a television. Being only four years old, I didn't yet know anything about Martin Luther King, Jr. or his famous *I Have a Dream* speech or anything else about inequality or injustice to black people. In fact, looking back on kindergarten through twelfth grade, I can only remember two examples of black people living in my hometown - one black family with children (one of whom was in my grade and became a close friend) and my first grade teacher, whom I dearly loved. I've often wondered since if perhaps she was the black lady I'd seen in line that day in the account given above.

Children are innocent and colorblind - unless someone teaches them differently. How often have you seen pictures of little children of different color and race holding hands and playing together or proclaiming to be *twins* because they are dressed in similar outfits? Their idea of beauty has more to do with someone's smile or kindness than their physical looks. I think of a story I heard as a child of a little boy looking for his mother. His description to the officer was that she was "the most beautiful woman in the world." When the boy finally found his mother and flung his arms around her neck, the officer was stunned because the woman was almost homely in appearance and plainly dressed. We need to have eyes like those of that little boy.

Innocent children want to have relationships with their loved ones. They want to draw or paint pictures for them or pick beautiful flowers (usually dandelions) to give to them. They want to *help* cook, clean, and serve. Their hearts are beautiful, pure, and good. They completely trust you, as their parent, to provide for their every need; in turn, they give you their *all*.

We, as parents or grandparents, want to cherish these wonderful times and use the opportunities God has given us to nurture these beautiful qualities. Heaven knows this window of innocence is small; so we display those pictures and bouquets of dandelions. Why? Because every child is a Michelangelo, and we love bouquets of weeds? Of course not! It's because we love our children or grandchildren and the beautifully generous hearts they have.

God is the same way with you. When you allow Him to adopt you into His family, you become *His* child. You offer Him your best, which is nothing compared to what He could provide for Himself; but He loves *you*, and so He loves your offerings!

In the gospels, Jesus teaches that you must become "child*like*" (not "child*ish*", which is quite the opposite) in order to be part of His Kingdom. You are *not* to copy the world's ideas or the so-called religious leaders' ideas as you might suppose, but to be pure in heart and mind and to totally trust in your Maker.

How you live and respond to people in life makes just as much, if not more, difference as the things you say. I'm sure you've heard the saying, "I'd rather see a sermon than hear one any day," and it couldn't be more true. YOU have the power to *choose* to promote peace, love, and unity.

Unfortunately, you are being bombarded daily by satan – whom Jesus described in the gospels as "the father of lies." The devil disguises himself as "an angel of light" while he is actually "like a roaring lion prowling around looking for someone to devour" (II Corinthians 11:14; I Peter 5:8). Much of what you see or hear in the media is skewed to lead you to believe that *all* of one particular race or occupation are bad because of a *few* who have made really bad choices. Make no mistake! The deceiver is the one behind all the hate and evil in this world.

Scripture tells us that we need to take a stand against the schemes of the devil. Because our fight is "not against flesh and blood, but against the rulers, authorities and powers of this dark world and against the spiritual forces of evil in the heavenly realms," we need to "put on the full armor of God" (Ephesians 6:11-12). I will go into this subject more fully in chapter 6, but suffice it to say, *you* have *choices*.

Is there hope for your family, your community, your nation, your world? Absolutely! Can YOU make a difference in all these areas? Yes! However, contrary to popular opinion, you do *not* have this power in and of yourself. Thankfully, you have been offered a gift, free of charge - the cornerstone to overcoming racism and prejudice of any kind.

Chapter 3

Relationship with God - Cornerstone to Overcoming Racism

A dam and Eve lived in perfect harmony and relationship with God as they watched over the Garden of Eden. They didn't have to pull weeds; they had no reason to fear wild animals or anything else. God told them they could eat of *any* of the beautiful and delicious fruit surrounding them, with only *one* exception – they were warned not to eat from the tree of knowledge of good and evil or they would die (Genesis Ch. 2). What a life! Who could want more?

But satan introduced doubt and discontent, just as he does today. At that time, the devil took on the form of a serpent and tempted Eve by twisting God's words and causing her to question God's intentions. The devil first asked Eve if God really said they *couldn't* eat *any* of the fruit in the garden. She quickly stood up for God, saying they could eat any of it except the fruit of the tree in the middle of the garden; they were not to even touch it or they would die. The deceiver convinced her that *not only* would they NOT die, *but* they would know everything and be *just like God* (Genesis Ch. 3).

Jesus' best friend John describes this and *all* temptation by saying that if we value worldly things (physical things we crave because they feel good, look good, and puff us up) more than we value our relationship with God, the Father's Love is not in us (I John 2:15-17). Isn't that what all sin boils down to? Things that *feel* good, things that *look* good, and our *pride*?

Adam and Eve did not physically die right on the spot; so did God lie? Absolutely not! They would eventually die physically (as will all of mankind), but they would suffer an even worse punishment than *physical* death; *spiritual* death was experienced immediately. The word *death* simply means *separation*. No longer could they walk and talk with God as they had from the beginning; they had destroyed their *relationship with Him*.

With their disobedience, sin entered the world; and they were physically banished from the Garden of Eden. Adam (and mankind in general) was now cursed with having to work hard because of thorns and weeds; Eve (and women ever after) would be cursed with pain in childbearing. They both would later endure excruciating pain when their older son Cain murdered his younger brother Abel due to jealousy. This is the first recorded example of a ruined *relationship between people*. In reality, Adam and Eve lost two sons that day because Abel was dead and Cain was banished; Cain became a wanderer for the rest of his life. Both sons were forever separated from them.

I share that illustration because you need to understand that you *need* Jesus to restore both that perfect relationship you want with the Father ***and*** with other people. Paul's letter to the Galatians tells us that the Old Law was meant to be our *tutor*; it was to show us our *need* for a Savior. Under the Old Law, even *one* sin separated you from God and brought death. So, if you *ever* told a lie, stole something from someone, used God's Name in vain, or disobeyed your parents – you deserved *death*! Your sins could be rolled forward temporarily through animal sacrifices, but they never *really* went away. God is just, which means He *cannot* ignore sin; but because He is also love, He provided the perfect sacrifice to *pay* for *our* sin. Isaiah tells us it's not because God isn't powerful enough to save you, but it's your *own* evil that *separates* you from Him (Isaiah 59:1-2).

In case you think you're not that bad because you're a pretty good person, check out Romans 3:23-24: "*All* have sinned and are *not good enough* for God's glory, and *all* need to be made right with God by His grace, which is a free gift. They *need* to be made *free from sin* through Jesus Christ."

You *cannot* fix this situation yourself! You need His help.

The Good News is that God had a plan from the very beginning. God *created* you; you were His, but you *chose* to become *enslaved to sin*. This is why He sent His Son Jesus to die on the cross - to pay for your sins. He offers to take away your sins forever and allow you to have a perfect relationship with Him again - but the choice is yours. He offers you this gift freely, but He also *always* offers you freedom of *choice*.

When I was a young child, a visiting preacher gave an illustration I would never forget. He pointed to a twelve-year-old boy (we'll call him Joe) and had him come up front. The minister then proceeded to offer Joe a five-dollar bill. At first Joe was reluctant, thinking this must be a trick or that he would have to do some crazy or embarrassing stunt; but at the minister's insistence that it was a free gift, he finally took it and returned to his seat with a huge grin on his face. When the rest of us younger kids saw that Joe hadn't had to do anything weird, we wished *we* had been chosen to receive this gift.

The preacher asked us if Joe had earned the money, which of course he hadn't. Then he asked if Joe would own it if he had refused to believe him and had not taken the money from his extended hand, which of course he would not. He went on to explain that God's offer of salvation through Jesus Christ and the indwelling of His Holy Spirit are extended to *each* and *every* one of us, free of charge. We must believe that we are sinners in need of salvation and accept this free gift on His terms, realizing there is *nothing* we can do to deserve it or earn it.

God has offered you forgiveness of your sins, allowing you to have renewed *relationship* with Him now here on earth and through all eternity in Heaven. He has also offered you the unlimited power of the Holy Spirit in your life. His power can *transform* you from an ugly caterpillar full of sin into a beautiful butterfly full of the life and light of Jesus Christ. His Spirit also *intercedes* for you in prayer and *enables* you to be an example to draw others to God (Acts 2:38; I Thessalonians 4:13-18; Romans 12:1-2; Romans 8:26-27; I Corinthians 11:1; Philippians 4:13; I John Ch. 1).

In response to Peter's sermon on the Day of Pentecost (Acts 2), those in the crowd who suddenly realized that *they* were responsible for sending Jesus to the cross were "cut to the heart" and cried out to him and the rest of the apostles, "Brothers, what shall we do?"

"Peter said to them, 'Change your hearts and lives and be baptized, each one of you, in the name of Jesus Christ for the forgiveness of your sins. And you *will receive* the gift of the Holy Spirit. This promise is *for you, for your children* [those Jewish by race and their descendants] and for *all who are far off* [non-Jews]. It is for *everyone* the Lord our God calls to Himself [*anyone* who hears and obeys the Gospel].'

Peter warned them with many other words. He begged them, 'Save yourselves from the evil of today's people!' Then those people who accepted what Peter said were baptized. About three thousand people were added to the number of believers that day" (Acts 2:38-41).

I want you to understand that God has given you *everything you need* to combat racism or any kind of prejudice today. Because you already have a personal relationship with the creator, you do not need to have miraculous gifts, to be famous, or to be a political figure. **Love** is all you need. The whole book of I John explains that *God is Love* and that He wants us to love one another. If you have obeyed God's will in faith, you have the *power of His Spirit living in you;* you also have the power of His Word – and that is enough. The famous love chapter of the Bible (I Corinthians 13) ends with this: "So these three things continue forever: faith, hope, and love. And the greatest of these is love."

The book of Acts gives many examples of people responding to the gospel message (the Good News) - people from all different backgrounds, people like you and me. It wasn't *just* those people listening on the Day of Pentecost who sent Jesus to the cross. It was *me;* it was *you*; it was *all* of us. God showed Peter and the rest of the Jewish believers that Gentiles (anyone who wasn't born a Jew) were *also* welcomed into His Kingdom, the Church (Acts Ch. 10 and 13).

In fact, "You were *all baptized* into Christ, and so you were *all clothed* with Christ. This means that you are *all children* of God through faith in Christ Jesus. In Christ, there is *no difference* between Jew and Greek, slave and free person, male and female. You are ***all the same*** in Christ Jesus. You *belong to* Christ, *so* you are Abraham's descendants. You will *inherit all* of God's blessings because of the promise ***God*** made to Abraham" (Galatians 3:26-29).

As you can see, God has extended this free gift of salvation to *you* and has promised that *His Spirit* will *live in* and *empower* you to do His will (I Corinthians 3:16; 6:19-20; 12:4-7,11,13,18-20,27). You can use this gift to make a difference in your own life and in the lives of others – some of whom you may not even know (just as the black lady in chapter one had an impact on me).

Jesus prayed for Himself, His apostles, and finally for *all* believers - like you - who believe through the message that His apostles and others shared through His inspired Word (the Bible). What did Jesus ask His Father for? That we ***all "may be one"*** in Him and the Father and that we be "brought to **complete unity**" so that the world would know that God sent Jesus (John 17:20-26 NIV).

How do you begin? The Bible tells us in Genesis that God created us in His image. He did not want puppets; He wanted *relationship,* so He gave us all the *freedom* of *choice*. Many people think they are too far gone, that they can't be forgiven for what they've done, or that God wouldn't want them; but Scripture tells us that God's *desire* is that *everyone* would come to repentance. He does **not** want **anyone** to be lost (II Peter 3:9).

The Bible tells us of God's love and His desire for *all* people to come back to Him in repentance so that each one of us can have perfect relationship with Him again, both now and for all eternity. His plan to save us was not an afterthought. He knew from the time of creation that a relationship with us would cost Him dearly because we could not be perfect on our own - It would cost Him His own Son. Yet, God still chose to give us the freedom of choice.

The Father, Son, and Holy Spirit (sometimes referred to as the Godhead, the Trinity, or the Triune God) are One God (Genesis Ch. 1; John Ch. 1). All were in unity at the time of creation. Through the Son's sacrifice on the cross, we can now be *reconciled* with our Father in heaven (Colossians Ch. 1). That means we have the opportunity to return to having a *perfect relationship* with God – one in which we are no longer separated from Him because of our sin. Now His Spirit lives in us and guides us in His ways. "But if we live in the light, as God is in the light, we can share fellowship with each other. Then the blood of Jesus, God's Son, cleanses us from every sin" (I John 1:7). What a life! Right?

*Do **not** allow* the devil to snatch this precious gift away by *tricking* you into believing his lies. In the Garden, he appeared as a serpent; today he uses more subtle disguises. The devil wants you to be hateful and mean, to think evil thoughts and be prejudiced. He wants you to choose his side, to become discouraged and give up on God. He wants you to rely on our *own* power instead of leaning on the Holy Spirit. Do **not** let him fool you. Do **not** let him win in your life. The deceiver *promises* happiness, but he *delivers* death instead.

As my husband Dewey used to always say: "Revelation tells us that God has *already* won; so if you're a Christian, *don't quit* and *don't change sides.* If you're not a Christian, *join* the winning team!"

You have been given a sneak preview to the end of time. No matter what happens in this life and no matter how things may *appear* to be going the devil's way, God has promised that He has already won.

We *can* have peace, love, and unity with God and with one another; but we *must* humble ourselves and cling to Him and *His* power (James 4:7-10). We *can* learn to be content in whatever circumstances we are in, but first we need to have a positive mindset (Philippians 4:11-13). Remember, Paul was writing from *prison* when he encouraged the Christians in Philippi to be joyful in all circumstances:

"Rejoice in the Lord always. I will say it again: Rejoice! Let your gentleness be evident to all. The Lord is near. Do not be anxious about anything, but in every situation, by prayer and petition, with thanksgiving, present your requests to God. And the peace of God, which transcends all understanding, will guard your hearts and your minds in Christ Jesus.

Finally, brothers, whatever is true, whatever is noble, whatever is right, whatever is pure, whatever is lovely, whatever is admirable – if anything is excellent or praiseworthy – think about such things. Whatever you have learned or received or heard from me, or seen in me – put it into practice. And the God of peace will be with you" (Philippians 4:4-9; NIV).

Paul prayed, "...that the God who gives hope will fill you with much joy and peace while you trust in Him. Then your hope will overflow by the *power* of the Holy Spirit"(Romans 15:13).

   ***   You
are being sent messages from the devil every day by what is trending in the world, but Jesus has other plans for you. James tells us, "You should know that loving the world is the same as hating God. Anyone who wants to be a friend of the world becomes God's enemy" (James 4:4). James is not saying we should not love *people*, but that we should not listen to the *philosophy* of the world:

- *The world tells you to "follow your heart"; **Jesus says, "Follow Me."***

- *The world says, "Be true to yourself"; **Jesus said, "Whoever wants to be My disciple must give up the things they want."***

- *The world says, "Believe in yourself"; **Jesus said, "Believe in Me."***

- *The world says, "Live your truth"; **Jesus said, "I Am the Truth."***

- *The world says, "Do unto others before they do unto you"; **Jesus said, "Do to others what you want them to do to you."***

- *The world says, "Raise yourself up by your own bootstraps"; **Scripture says, "Don't be too proud in the Lord's Presence, and He will lift you up."***

- *The world says, "Sell yourself so you get credit from people"; **Jesus said, "When you do good, don't let anyone know what you are doing .... He will reward you."***

- *The world says, "All roads lead to heaven"; **Jesus said, "I Am the Way ... the only Way to the Father is through Me."***

- *The world says, "As long as you're happy"; **Jesus said, "What will it profit a man if he gains the whole world and loses his soul?"***

- *The world says, "Love only those who love you"; **Jesus said, "Love your enemies and pray for those who hurt you."***

- *The world says, "You are valued by your status"; **Jesus said, "Whoever is your servant is the greatest among you."***

This list could go on and on, but you get the point (Matthew 5:43-44; 7:12; 16:24-26; 23:11; Mark 8:36; Luke 14:10; John 11:26; 14:6; James 4:10).

We've seen how to have *relationship* with God and that His power is *essential* in fighting racism and prejudice; next we'll see that God wants to adopt *you* as His own child, *no matter* your color, gender, occupation, race, or background.

Chapter 4

God Wants to Adopt You, Regardless of Your Race

With the exception of the death of Dewey's dad the month following our wedding, everything was wonderful at first. We each were one of five children, and we wanted to have several children of our own; so Dewey purchased an insurance plan that would cover pregnancy. We were busy and happy, but we longed to be parents. Months passed and each time I was late, we would get all excited and do a pregnancy test; but we never got the results we hoped for.

Family members were having babies; and although we were happy for them, we were discouraged ourselves. After eight months in upstate New York, we moved to Southern Wyoming, where Dewey would have his own ministry. After moving there, we finally sought medical help and found out we *could not* have children. Dewey was especially devastated.

When I was younger, I had seen shows about couples who had children and then adopted; so although I was upset that I could never physically carry Dewey's child, I was already very open to adoption. Dewey, on the other hand, had never even had the *idea* of adoption cross his mind. He had always just thought, you get married and have kids – simple as that. At first he was afraid that he might not love an adopted child as much as one of his own flesh and blood; so until he was able to wrap his head around the idea, we didn't even pursue it.

When he was ready, we began the process. It felt as if we had to jump through a million hoops and wait forever! On the application and for the profile, we had to answer all kinds of personal questions, making us feel very vulnerable; so it was especially hard to hear of women who *didn't* even *want* to be moms getting pregnant - or *worse*, to see parents being abusive to the children they'd *already* been blessed with! None of *those* people had to fill out paperwork telling their whole life story or have background checks done or anything else to have a child, while here we were wanting a child so badly we would jump through all kinds of hoops to have him/her in our family. Anyone who has gone through this process understands the emotional ups and downs we experienced.

We finally got the call from our adoption agency in Colorado in the spring of 1989; we were so excited! When Dewey first held our beautiful baby boy whose birth mother had chosen us from our adoption profile in spite of our lower income, he never again wondered if he could love this child as much as one of his own flesh and blood. We named him Joshua Caleb and hoped that he too would grow up to be *strong and courageous,* as Moses had encouraged his namesake to be. We were overjoyed to be able to call Joshua our son.

About two years later, we had a baby girl in our home for a few weeks (as a foster child) with intention to adopt; but the birth mother changed her mind. We were devastated to have to take her back. That was one of the hardest things we ever had to endure. To us, it was *like* the *death* of a child because we would *forever* be *separated* from her and never know what happened to her. As with other trials, I knew God was always there to comfort us; and I dreamed that someday that little girl would hear the Gospel and share it with her whole birth family. Knowing God is in control gives me *peace.* (Romans 8:28; II Thessalonians 3:3; I Timothy 4:6,8; II Timothy 1:11-14; I Peter 1:4-7).

Later that same year, we would be allowed to adopt another baby boy; we named our second son David Joseph (named for both "the man after God's Own heart" and the man God would use to preserve His people in Egypt). A few years later when we lived in Washington State, we adopted twin girls. We named them Beth Marie (derivatives of Elizabeth, relative of Mary - and Mary, mother of our Lord) and Charity Marie (King James word for love and again a form of Mary). Our hearts were full and content. In addition to our two sons, we now had two beautiful daughters; and we were basking in the love of God. God blessed our lives so much through these four wonderful people, and we gained a deeper understanding of God and how much He loves us and wants to adopt us.

<hr />

God *chose us* to be adopted as *His* children through the blood of Jesus Christ *before* He even created the world! (Ephesians 1). Why would He do that, knowing that we would sin and fall short of His glory and that it would cost Him the life of His Son Jesus? Let's take a step back to the Old Testament. God already owned the whole world and everything in it. He didn't *need* anything from His chosen people of that day (the Israelites) – He *wanted* **relationship**. He did not choose them because they were a powerful nation or because they were such good people. He chose them because of His love for and promises to Abraham, Isaac, and Jacob. He wanted these people to have *relationship* with Him and to obey His laws for their *own* good!

Who does God choose today? Only the beautiful and smart? Only the powerful or rich? Only those of a particular gender, color, or race? No. God chose to give His Son as a ransom for *all* who would trust and obey – anyone who would *choose* to follow Him! In fact, God chose what the world thought had *no* value and gave us *His* value so that no one could boast (I Corinthians 1:26-31).

God gave us His creation, His Word, and His Son to show us who He is – to show us how powerful and mighty He is, and yet how much He loves us and wants a relationship with each of us. Then, He gave us the *free choice* of whether to follow Him or to remain enslaved by the power of darkness. Just as Dewey and I wanted to love and nurture our adopted children and offer them opportunities and relationships that their birth parents may have wanted for them but couldn't offer at the time, God wants to give us His kingdom and blessings, along with His own Son - Jesus Christ! (Luke 12:32, Romans 8:17). God offers us so much more than we, as parents, ever could offer our children; yet *He still lets us choose* to allow Him to adopt us.

Let's take a little journey through Biblical history. Even though God had a *plan* for us since the very beginning, the Old Testament shows how God first preserved the human race during the flood through the faith and obedience of Noah and his family. Later, He preserved His chosen people because of His relationship with Abraham and the promises He had made to him and his son Isaac and grandson Jacob. God promised a *land* to Abraham's descendants (who, God said, would be as numerous as the stars in the sky- even though Abraham and his wife were both old and past the age of childbearing at that time). God also promised a *Messiah* who would rule an *everlasting* kingdom would come from Abraham's descendants.

Abraham's grandson Jacob (later called Israel) had a son named Joseph, whom God used to preserve the Israelites through a famine by raising him to be second in command to the Pharaoh of Egypt. Years later, another Pharaoh arose, one who knew nothing about Joseph. When he came into power, he made slaves of God's chosen people because they had become quite numerous; he was afraid they would turn against the Egyptians. When they continued to multiply, he demanded that all the male children be exposed to the elements and the Nile River. Yet God continued to protect His people.

During that time, a man and woman from the tribe of Levi had a son they hid for as long as they could (about three months). Finally, his mother made a tar-covered basket of reeds that would float, put the baby in the basket, and set it among the tall grass at the edge of the Nile River. The baby's big sister (Miriam) stayed close by to see what would happen. Pharaoh's daughter came to the river to bathe and seeing the basket, sent her slave girl to get it. When she opened the basket, she realized the beautiful baby boy was one of the Hebrew babies. He was crying, and she felt sorry for him. Miriam seized the opportunity and offered to find a Hebrew woman to nurse the baby for the princess, and she agreed! Miriam brought back her own mother be a nursemaid for the baby, and the princess said she would pay her to take care of him. We aren't told how long his own mother was able to teach him and guide him, but that "when the child grew older," his mother took him to the princess, who adopted him as her own son. Because she had pulled him out of the water, the princess named him Moses (which sounds like the Hebrew word for *to pull out)*.

In the New Testament, the writer of Hebrews (Ch. 11) tells us that when Moses grew up, he *chose* to follow God and to suffer with His people for the sake of the promised Christ rather than to have the temporary physical pleasures and privileges he had previously enjoyed as a son of Pharaoh's daughter.

Looking back to the book of Exodus in the Old Testament, we see that when Moses became a man, he tried to protect his people, to be a leader for them; but after he realized someone had witnessed his slaying an Egyptian while trying to defend an Israelite, he ran away to a distant land (Midian).

Forty years later, God called Moses from a burning bush. Moses didn't think he had the ability to do what God asked of him because he had tried earlier but failed and because he had a speech problem. After God reminded Moses that He is the One who *made* the tongue, He allowed Moses' brother Aaron to return to Egypt with him to be his voice. God then led His people out of the land of Egypt after demonstrating His mighty power to Egypt and to all the known world through ten plagues.

God talked with His friend Moses, and He gave His Law to the people of Israel through him. God made it clear that He had chosen the Israelites because of His relationship and promises to their ancestors, *not* because of their *own* might or their *own* goodness. They were to *separate* themselves from the evil ways of the world and to be a *living* picture of the kind of relationship God wants with His people. The Old Testament prophet Malachi tells us that God's people had broken the Law by intermarrying with the peoples of the lands they conquered (Malachi Ch. 2). This law was given not because those other nations were different colors or races, but because the Israelites would be tempted to worship false gods and do the very things God hated. Unfortunately, the nation of Israel as a whole vacillated between being *elitists* who thought they were *better than* everyone else and being *conformists* who wanted to be *just like* everyone else!

Hebrews chapter 11, known to some as "the Hall of Faith," lists Noah, Abraham, Moses, and many others who obeyed God in faith, but who (the writer tells us) never *saw* the fulfillment of God's promises - except through the eyes of faith. But now, we see those promises were fulfilled. Paul explains in the book of Romans that now the term "Jew" refers to *all* those who *choose* to fully follow Christ in a *spiritual* sense, as opposed to those who were merely *physically* born of the Jewish race (Romans 2:29).

Paul describes the rich and glorious spiritual blessings we have in Christ – all because of *God's* love, grace, and mercy offered through the sacrifice Christ Jesus made for us. He gave us His Spirit as a guarantee that one day we will receive everything that He has promised us (Ephesians Ch. 1).

Paul continues by saying that we (non-Jews) *were* spiritually *dead*, but *now* we have *life*. He says we had been living like the world, ruled by evil powers. Paul then connects with them (and us) by including himself and his Jewish brethren when he says, "In the past, *all of us* lived like them, trying to please our sinful selves and doing all the things our bodies and minds wanted. We should have suffered God's anger because of the way we were. We were the same as all other people." He goes on to say that salvation was given as a *free gift* of God to *all* of us "so that for all future time He could show the very great riches of His grace by being kind to us in Christ Jesus." Now we have *purpose:* "God has made us what we are. In Christ Jesus, God made us to do good works, which God planned in advance for us to live our lives doing" (Ephesians 2:1,3,6-10).

Next, Paul says that although we non-Jews formerly "had no hope, and ... did not know God," we who *were far away* from being able to have a relationship with God are now *drawn close* to Him and can enjoy the same promises the Jews (God's chosen people) had been given years before. "Christ Himself is our *peace"* (Ephesians 2:12-14a).

Christ's purpose (and the mystery to which Paul keeps referring in the book of Ephesians) is then revealed: God sent His Son (Jesus) to end the Old Law and to *save all* of us from our sins, allowing us to have (a vertical) *relationship with Him.* He also "broke down that wall of hate" between the Jews and the Gentiles (anyone not of the Jewish race), so He could "make the two groups of people become *one new people* in Him and in this way make peace (a horizontal *relationship between people* of any race). It was also Christ's purpose to end the hatred between the two groups, to make them into one body and to bring them back to God. Christ did all this with His death on the cross.... Yes, it is through Christ we all have the right to come to the Father in one Spirit" (Ephesians 2:14-16, 18).

Paul ends this chapter by describing us *all* as "*belonging to* God's family ... a *united* people in *one* body ... *citizens* together with God's holy people." We are "*like a building* that was built on the foundation of the apostles and prophets," with Christ being "the most important Stone ... Who holds it all together.... He makes it grow and become a *holy temple* in the Lord. And in Christ you, too, are being *built together* with the Jews into a place where God lives through the Spirit"

(Ephesians 2:14-22).

Through the four Gospel accounts (Matthew, Mark, Luke, and John) and the book of Galatians you can see how Jesus *fulfilled* all the Old Law and agreement between God and His people. The author of Hebrews also shows us how Jesus was *superior* to the prophets, angels, sacrifices, priests, and Moses and that He gave us a *New* Agreement by taking away our sins once for all time. The author then shows us that we are to follow those "Hall of Famers" of faith that were given earlier (Hebrews Ch. 11) and ultimately Christ's perfect example to never give up, even when suffering. The writer reminds us that God is our Father and that sometimes our suffering is His discipline – proof that He loves us as His children (Hebrews 12:5-11).

***

So now, we have taken a quick journey through the Old Testament and have seen how Abraham showed us faith and Moses brought us the Law. Then we went into the New Testament to see how none of us can be right with God in and of ourselves, but that because of His love, grace, and mercy, *He* sent Jesus to *give* us the free gift of *forgiveness, salvation,* and eternal *relationship* with Him through adoption as His children, regardless of our ancestry. He has given us His *peace,* a *purpose,* and the *power* to accomplish His will through His Holy Spirit.

So, what's *your part* in solving the problem of racism and prejudice? I recently read an anonymous quote that said: "The only thing I can do about awful people is not be one of them." I thought it was cute, but I think you'll see in the coming chapters that there's much more.

Chapter 5

What's Your Part in the Solution to Racism/Prejudice?

The army officers all dreaded coming to this meeting called by their king, the mighty King of Aram. Was he going to send them to set up *another* camp? They all knew that he was probably furious because they had been at war with Israel for a long time now, but they still had nothing to show for it. They had followed all of the king's directions exactly. It wasn't *their* fault that several times now he had told them to set up camp against Israel in many different places, always with the same results. Nobody from Israel had come that way once they had set up camp; the king's plans had been thwarted every time. It was almost as if the Israelites *knew* to avoid every place he chose.

It really didn't matter who was at fault, though. The Aramean king was known for his fierce anger and his cruel ways to punish anyone who stood in his way. So although they knew they dare not waste any time getting to the appointed meeting place, their feet felt like lead; their heads were bowed down with fear; and instead of voices, one could hear the clank of armor as each came to his place.

Finally, the dreaded moment arrived. Their king's face was contorted with anger as he faced the officers he had called together. "Which of you is working for the king of Israel? Every time we set up camp, one of you has warned him; so nobody comes that way!"

All of the officers looked at one another in fear and disbelief. They each knew that if anyone had been so traitorous, the king would have him tortured and killed on the spot. If *nobody* confessed, the king would use his *own* judgment to decide who was guilty.

To everyone's amazement, one of the officers spoke up, "It wasn't any of us, Master! It's Elisha, the prophet of Israel. He can tell you what you speak in your bedroom."

"Then go find him!" the king bellowed.

The king's men hurried out with a large army to follow his orders, eager to be as far away from the king's anger as possible. Only the officer who spoke up *really* knew whether his explanation was true, but the king seemed to buy it; so nobody was complaining. They wasted no time finding where Elisha was staying and surrounded the city that very night.

Elisha's servant got up early in the morning and went outside to greet the day. This was his favorite time of day. He could enjoy the Lord's creation and give Him a prayer of thanks, maybe even sing one of the Psalms of David. His duties for Elisha wouldn't begin until his master awakened.

He hadn't been outside long when the hair stood up on the back of his neck; he felt he was being watched. Suddenly, he realized the city was completely surrounded by the enemy army on horseback. There were so many Arameans! How could he and Elisha possibly defend themselves?! He cried out to Elisha, "Oh, my master, what can we do?"

"Elisha said, 'Don't be afraid. The army that fights for us is larger than the one against us.' Then Elisha prayed, 'Lord, open my servant's eyes, and let him see.'

The Lord opened the eyes of the young man, and he saw that the mountain was full of horses and chariots of fire all around Elisha" (paraphrased II Kings 6:8-15a; quoted vs.12b and 15b-17).

I share that story from II Kings 6 to remind you that the **power** for change rests in God. In case you are wondering if we still have that power today, Jesus' Apostle John assures us we do. "My dear children, you belong to God and have defeated them [enemies of Christ] because God's Spirit, who is *in you*, is *greater* than the devil, who is in the world" (I John 4:4).

***

My husband Dewey used to use a car battery to illustrate that although we, as Christians, have the power of God's Spirit within us (like a good battery in a car), if we *lose connection*, that power will *not* be available to us. The Spirit's power flows from God to us mostly through His Word, but sometimes through random people, situations, or thoughts that seem to come out of nowhere. We are to "test" these spirits to make sure they are remaining true to God's Word. In turn, we pour our hearts out to God in prayer, and He is faithful to answer our prayers. But what happens if we are so busy and distracted that we neglect our relationship with God? That would be like the wires to the car being disconnected from the car's battery. If we allow sin to consume us and build up around our hearts, that too can keep us from the Spirit's power, just like corrosion can disrupt the connection to the car's battery. Note that *any* disconnect problem is with *us*, not God. He is all-powerful.

Paul explains how we can be part of the **solution** to racism and prejudice, by showing us how to live in the love and unity found in Christ (Ephesians Ch. 3-6). Paul starts by sharing this powerful prayer for the people of that day - and for all of us who are now children adopted by our Heavenly Father:

"I ask the Father in His great glory to give you the power to be strong inwardly through His Spirit. I pray that Christ will live in your hearts by faith and that your life will be strong in love and be built on love. And I pray that you and all God's holy people will have the power to understand the greatness of Christ's love – how wide and how long and how high and how deep that love is. Christ's love is greater than anyone can ever know, but I pray that you will be able to know that love. Then you can be filled with the fullness of God. With God's power working in us, God can do much, much more than anything we can ask or imagine. To Him be the glory in the church and in Christ Jesus for all time, forever and ever. Amen" (Ephesians 3:16-21).

Did you catch all that?! Paul prays that we will **understand** Christ's incomprehensible love. He knows the more we understand God's great love (God: the Father, Son, and Spirit), the more it will naturally pour out of our lives towards others. Because of God's love for us, His power through us can accomplish much, much more than we could *possibly* think or imagine! I don't know about you, but as evidenced in chapter one of this book, I can dream pretty big.

Paul continues to describe the life of light and unity that can be ours, but also gives us a hint of the part we play in this scenario. Look at Ephesians 4:2-3: "Always *be* humble, gentle, and patient, accepting each other in love. You are joined together with *peace* through the Spirit, so make every effort to continue together in this way." *Humble? Gentle? Patient? Accepting and loving?* Yes! God called us out of the worldly way of thinking to *be like Jesus*!

In his letter to the Philippians, Paul encourages us to **imitate** Jesus, who totally **humbled** Himself to become a man and live in complete obedience to God. You cannot imagine how much love Jesus showed by doing that. He had it *all*, yet was willing to give up everything for a time, to pay the ransom for your soul – because He loves you! (Philippians 2).

So how are you to live? You are to "leave your **old self** - to stop living the evil way you lived before." You are "to be **made new** in your hearts, to become a **new person**." You are "**made** to be truly *good* and *holy*" (Ephesians 4:22-23).

In the previous chapter on adoption, I referred to the book of Hebrews. In Hebrews chapters 12 and 13, the writer tells us to be careful *how we live* now that we understand that God is our Father. Because of this new relationship, we are to:

- *"Try to live in peace with all people, and try to live free from sin."*

- *"Be careful that no one fails to receive God's grace and begins to cause trouble among you."*

- *"So, be careful and do not refuse to listen when God speaks."*

- *"So, let us be thankful, because we have a kingdom that cannot be shaken."*

- *"Worship God in a way that pleases Him with respect and fear."*

- *"Keep on loving each other as brothers and sisters."*

- *"Remember to welcome strangers, because some who have done this have welcomed angels without knowing it."*

- *"Remember those who are in prison as if you were in prison with them."*

- *"Remember those who are suffering as if you were suffering with them."*

- *"Marriage should be honored by everyone, and husband and wife should keep their marriage pure."*

- *"Remember your leaders who taught God's message to you....and copy their faith."*

- *"Keep your lives free from the love of money, and be satisfied with what you have."*

- *"Do not let all kinds of strange teachings lead you into the wrong way."*

- *"So, through Jesus let us offer to God our sacrifice of praise."*

- *"Obey your leaders and act under their authority."*

- *"Do not forget to do good to others, and to share with them."*

- *"Pray for us."*

(Hebrews 12:14-15,25,28; 13:1-5,7,9,15-18)

The above list from Hebrews is not exhaustive, and it might be a challenge to memorize. Remember this: Jesus basically summed up *all* Biblical teaching when He said that loving God with everything you've got is **the** most important thing in life; the **second** most important thing is loving/treating others the way He first loved/ treated you (Mark 12:29-31; John 13:34).

If you have a thankful attitude for the love, mercy, and grace God has freely given you, won't you be more apt to love and forgive others? Won't it make you desire to please God by following Him and worshiping Him

the way He wants of you? The Father wants us to empathize with others –
as if we were in their place. Consider the parable Jesus told of the *prodigal
son.* You see that the father welcomed his son back, no questions asked.
The older brother did not understand his own blessings; therefore, he
refused to forgive (Luke 15:11-32). Jesus told another parable of a rich
man who forgave a huge debt to one of his servants, but the forgiven
servant then refused to forgive a small debt owed him by a fellow servant.
Why? Because he did not really understand that his *own* debt had been
completely forgiven (Matthew 18:21-35). Are you beginning to see the
connections and the part you play in the solution to the problem of racism
and prejudice?

The last part of Ephesians chapter four and the first half of chapter five, I
call "Putting Off and Putting On" because Paul shows us some practical
things we need to take out of our lives and then gives practical suggestions
on how to fill those voids.

   Put off: lying; *Put on: telling each other the truth..*   **Put off:**
letting the devil defeat you because of your anger; *Put on: forgiveness.*

   Put off: stealing; *Put on: working, which provides an honest
living for oneself and provides something to share with others who
are poor.*

   Put off: words that hurt others; *Put on: words that build up and
encourage others, making them stronger..*

   Put off: making the Spirit sad with bitterness, anger, evil words and
actions; *Put on: being kind, loving, and forgiving - like Christ.*

Put off: sexual sin, any kind of evil or greed (which he says is serving a false god), any evil or foolish talk or evil jokes; ***Put on: holiness, giving thanks to God, obeying Him, learning what pleases Him, living right and wisely, and making the most of every opportunity to do good.***

Put off: getting drunk with wine; ***Put on: being filled with the Spirit, singing psalms, hymns and spiritual songs to each other and to God.***

Jesus taught that we will find ourselves in a worse state than we were in before if we do not fill the void with good - the void left from our past evil ways (Matthew 12:43-45). That's why putting off evil and replacing it with good is so important. The apostle Paul says, "You are God's children whom He loves, so try to be like Him. Live a life of love, just as Christ loved us and gave Himself for us as a sweet-smelling offering and sacrifice to God.... In the *past* you were full of darkness, but *now* you are full of light in the Lord. So live like children who belong to the light. Light brings every kind of goodness, right living, and truth" (Ephesians 5:1-2,8-9).

In the book of Galatians, Paul also teaches about the need to get rid of sin in our lives so that we can be *filled with* and be *led by* the **Spirit**. He warns us about the daily struggle going on within each of us Christians – the **fight** between our *human* nature and *God's* Spirit. Paul says that several things the sinful self does are obvious: sexual sins, worshiping false gods, practicing witchcraft, being drunk, and having wild and wasteful parties; *but this list **also includes** hating, making trouble, being jealous,* *being angry, being selfish, making people angry with each other, causing divisions among people, and feeling envy.* Several of those sound like *racism*, don't they? We tend to categorize sin into little or big sins, but Paul does **not** differentiate when he says that "those who do these things will *not* inherit God's kingdom" (Galatians 5:19-21). We have *died* to that old way of living for ourselves; if we follow the Spirit, we *will* have a "new life." The Spirit produces fruit in us, replacing the evil things in our lives (Galatians 5:22-23); but I will go into that more in chapter seven of this book.

Maybe you feel you can never be forgiven for your past, much less make a difference now. I think I Corinthians 6:9-11 is one of the most encouraging scriptures because Paul describes several people whose *practices* would have kept them out of God's kingdom; he says that some of these people **used to be** this way, but then they were made *clean* and *right* with God. The world would have you believe you were born with sin and that because of this, you cannot change; but listen to this: "Surely you know that the people who *do* wrong will not inherit God's kingdom. Do not be fooled. Those who sin sexually, worship idols, take part in adultery, those who are male prostitutes, or men who have sexual relations with other men, those who steal, are greedy, get drunk, lie about others, or rob – these people will not inherit God's kingdom. *In the **past**, some of you **were** like that, but you were **washed** clean.* You were **made holy**, and you were **made right** with God in the Name of the Lord Jesus Christ and in the Spirit of our God." None of us is exempt; God hates sin, but He **loves** the sinner and wants **all** of us to reap the benefits of a new life in Christ (Read Ephesians 2:1-10).

Off with the old way of life and on with the new; no matter your past, you can have **hope**! Jesus makes you complete. *Now you are set apart to do **good***.

Living life in the Light as God has called you to live *will* make a difference in this world. To those who are searching and want to do right, you will bring hope and will serve as an example – a *sweet* smell. To others, who **refuse** to listen to and obey God, you will be a light that exposes darkness – the *stench* of death to them (II Corinthians 2:14-17). While Jesus broke down the barriers of race and status, the division may *seem* even greater between those who follow Jesus' teachings and those who refuse to obey. However, the believer is called to **love** *unconditionally* as God loves us and to "Do your best to *live in peace* with everyone" (Romans 12:18).

The apostle Peter tells us, "But you are a chosen people, royal priests, a holy nation, a people for God's own possession. You were chosen to tell about the wonderful acts of God, who called you out of darkness into His wonderful light" (I Peter 2:9). He also begs us to avoid the evil things our bodies want to do and live such good lives that unbelievers around us "will see the good things you do and will give glory to God on the day when Christ comes again" (I Peter 2:11-12). He goes on to show that we are to submit to earthly authorities, giving them respect and honor because they were *meant* to punish evil and reward right actions. We are told, "It is God's desire that by doing good you should stop foolish people from saying stupid things about you" (I Peter 2:15). [Note: God allowed evil Roman emperors to rule during the time Peter was writing, but Christians were still encouraged to obey the laws of the land as long as they were not in opposition to God's laws.]

The apostles Paul and Peter each give us some practical advice about **how to** *live* as husbands and wives, children, fathers, masters and slaves (referring to the culture of the time), Christians towards one another - and even towards unbelievers, some of whom will treat you unfairly (Ephesians 5:21-6:9; I Peter Ch. 2-5). If you follow these instructions, you will definitely reap the benefits – some physical, some spiritual.

Paul says a husband is to love his wife *as Christ loved the church* – sacrificially, treating her like a bride in all her beauty, and caring for her as he cares for himself (Ephesians 5:25-33). Peter adds that a husband is to treat his wife with understanding, realizing that she is weaker, and to show her respect because God blesses them both with the same grace (I Peter 3:7). [Note: Peter's instructions in I Peter 3:1-7 begin with the words, "In the same way," and follow the **example** of how Jesus first loved us, as shown in I Peter 2!] It's interesting to me that studies today show that a woman's deepest need is **love,** followed closely by **security** – of course God knew that all along.

Paul says a wife is to submit to her husband, giving him *respect* as the head of the family, just as Christ is the head of the church. Again, modern studies show that a man's greatest needs are **honor** and **respect.** Who knew? Peter encourages believing women who are married to unbelievers by reminding them that *some* husbands "...will *be persuaded* to believe *without* anyone's saying *a word* to them. They will be persuaded by the way their wives live. Your husbands will see the pure lives you live with your respect for God." Peter goes on to say that a woman's beauty should not merely reflect outward appearance, but "...should come from within - the beauty of a gentle and quiet spirit that will never be destroyed and is very precious to God" (I Peter 2:1-2,4). No nagging, preaching, yelling, or ignoring; instead be a Christ-like example. I have seen this in real life couples, and it is exciting and beautiful to behold.

Paul says children are to obey their parents, not only because it's the right thing to do, but that it is also the first command containing a promise: "Then everything will be well with you, and you will have a long life on the earth" (Ephesians 6:3).

Paul goes on to say that fathers are *not* to *exasperate* their children, "...but raise them in the *training* and *teaching* of the Lord" (Ephesians 6:4). I really believe this has to do with "walking the walk," not just, "talking the talk." Do not automatically expect your children to follow in your footsteps, having the same interests or talents that you have, but rather teach and train to the standard of Jesus for your children's character. Lead by example, encouraging them to be *their* best in their strong suits.

Again, because the slave/master passages refer to a time and culture in history long ago, you should think of a modern day application; think employee/employer and see how you can apply these teachings. Paul said slaves (employees) should respectfully obey their masters (employers) *even* when they aren't watching, just as if they were serving Jesus Himself (Ephesians 6:5-8). Peter said slaves (employees) should treat their masters (employers) "...with all *respect, not only* those who are good and kind, *but also* those who are dishonest. A person might have to suffer even when it is unfair, but if he thinks of God and can stand the pain, God is pleased" (I Peter 2:18-19). His reasoning? "This is what you were *called to do*, because *Christ* suffered for you and gave you an *example* to follow. So you *should do* as He did" (I Peter 2:21).

Paul said that lords/masters (employers) were to be good to their ser-vants/slaves (employees), realizing that God is *their* Lord/Master and that

He treats *everyone alike*! [Note: In the Old Testament, Jewish Law demanded that Hebrew slaves who had sold themselves to one of their countrymen to pay off a debt were to be *set free* every seventh year. At that time, he/she was to be given some of the master's flocks of animals, grain, and wine so that he/she could have a fresh start. However, if the slave *loved* his/her master, had a good life with the family, and *wanted* to stay, he/she would have his/her ear pierced with an awl and *chose* to be a slave for life (Deuteronomy 15:12-18). In a similar way, I *chose* to make Jesus my Lord/Master instead of being a slave to sin/satan. God lets us *choose* life!]

"Finally, *all* of you should be in agreement, understanding each other, loving each other as family, being kind and humble. Do not do wrong to repay a wrong, and do not insult to repay an insult. But repay with a blessing." - "If you are trying hard to do good, no one can really hurt you. But even if you suffer for doing right, you are blessed." Peter went on to tell us that Christ suffered for our sins, even though He was not guilty. His *body* was killed, but His *Spirit* lives on (I Peter 3:8-9a,13-14a,18).

Can you imagine what an impact we could make if we would truly follow these teachings in all our different walks of life? Change begins with *each* of *us* - every individual. When we "love our enemies" and "pray for those who persecute us" as Jesus taught in His Sermon On the Mount (Matthew Ch. 5), God will do amazing things. What would happen if when *you* were insulted, *you chose* to do something nice for that person in return? What if *all* Christians lived the way we are called to live?

In the past, you may have been *manipulated* to believe lies about others who are different from you. You may have been convinced that a particular person or group of people (distinguished by color, race, gender, abilities, interests, etc.) is your enemy. However, in the next chapter, I will share with you how the devil is the *real* enemy and *how to fight* against him and *protect yourself* from his racist schemes by using "the full armor of God."

Chapter 6

Protect Yourself from Satan's Racist Schemes - Use the Full Armor of God

Three-year-old Tommy was having so much fun jumping off the couch into his young father's waiting arms. His face was flushed, he was breathing hard, and little drops of sweat were running down his face; but none of that stopped him. They had been playing for awhile, and he was having the time of his life! Most importantly, Mommy wasn't there to tell him to get off the furniture!

"Okay," Daddy said in a slow, measured tone. "Now I'm going to take a step back so you can jump farther."

Tommy took that leap of faith each time Daddy stepped back, and Daddy caught him every time. He was getting pretty confident now, even though Daddy was already quite far from the couch.

"Ready?" Daddy asked. As Tommy nodded, Daddy shouted, "Jump!"

Tommy launched into the air, but suddenly he noticed that Daddy stepped back even farther and didn't even have his arms up to catch him! Little Tommy's arms flailed as he called out to his dad in terror, the ground rushing to meet him; but the face in front of him did not look like his dad any more. The last thing he remembered as his face hit the floor and everything went black was that his dad was laughing hysterically....

I am happy to inform you that the story above was totally made up. But, if you're like me, you found yourself hating that man – not just what the man had done. How could he have been so cruel to his own child – to build up his confidence, just to dash it to pieces?! But friends, that is exactly what the devil does to you. He entices you with little indiscretions and lets you get away with them until you are deeply involved and trapped in evil or dangerous things, and then whomp! He yanks the rug out from under you. He feels no remorse; rather, he leaves you to crash and burn and then laughs hysterically at your feeble, crumpled, and bloody self. He desperately wants you to fail. Why? Because he has *already* tried to overthrow the Almighty - but God won, hands down. You've heard the saying, "misery loves company." Since the devil can**not** defeat God, he wants to be *a god* to as many people as he can and take them down with him. He wants you to feel helpless and alone and defeated. He wants you to get distracted and *blame* someone else for all the evil in this world – to place blame on some *person* or *group* - or even *God!* How easy it is for him to accomplish this feat - to get us to turn against one another. He does not fight fairly! He uses skin color, religion, race, gender, and even our past to muddy the waters. He is determined to divide and conquer, and he is very good at it.

The **good** news is that God already knows how the devil works. God has *already* won the war between good and evil; not only that, He has given *you* the spiritual armor you need to *defend* yourself against the devil's wily schemes. The apostle Paul tells us:

"Finally, be strong in the Lord and in His great power. Put on the full armor of God so that you can **fight** against the devil's evil tricks. Our fight is *not* against people on earth but against the rulers and authorities and the powers of this world's darkness, against the spiritual powers of evil in the heavenly world" (Ephesians 6:10-12).

If we put on this armor every day, Paul admonishes us that we will make it through the whole fight and still be "standing strong." So what is this armor and what does it do? Let's discuss it piece by piece.

***

- THE BELT OF TRUTH

The Gospel of John describes Jesus as the Son of God, the "Word" who "became human and dwelt among us" and "was full of grace and truth" (John 1:14,17-18). Jesus said of Himself, "I *Am* the Way, and the Truth, and the Life. The only way to the Father is through Me" (John 14:6). To comfort His disciples regarding His coming death, Jesus promised to send "the Helper" who is "the Spirit of Truth" (John 15:26). Finally, as Jesus was praying to the Father for His followers, He said, "Make them ready for your service through your truth; your *teaching* is truth" (John 17:17).

So, how do you "put on" the belt of truth? Paul tells us, "But clothe yourselves with the Lord Jesus Christ, and forget about satisfying your sinful self" (Romans 13:14). "You were all baptized into Christ, and so you were all *clothed* with Christ. This means that you are all children of God through faith in Christ Jesus" (Galatians 3:26-27). We read about Jesus and His teachings through the Bible, and we put what we learn into practice. The more of His Word we incorporate into our hearts, our minds, and our actions, the better equipped we will be.

With every temptation, God provides a way of escape (I Corinthians 10:13). Jesus Himself showed us the perfect way to defend against satan, using the belt of truth. He used Scripture to combat *every* temptation the devil threw at Him in the wilderness following His baptism. In each temptation, Jesus answered the devil by saying, "It is written in Scripture..." and then quoted the Scripture with which He had armed Himself. The devil even tried taking a Scripture out of context and using it in a temptation! The devil led Jesus to a high place of the Temple in Jerusalem, saying, "If you are the Son of God, jump down, because it is written in the Scriptures: 'He has put His angels in charge of you. They will catch you in their hands so that you will not hit your foot on a rock'" (Psalm 91:11-12). Instead of falling for that, Jesus *recognized* the Scripture in context and answered with one that *did* apply. "It also says in the Scriptures, 'Do not test the Lord your God'" (Jesus quoted from Deuteronomy 6:16).

Jesus had invested time and effort to memorize God's written Word that was available to Him and all the Jewish people at that time. Now we have "the rest of the story" available - both the Old Testament and the New Testament in the Bible. I'm not suggesting that you need to memorize everything, but you do need to appreciate the privilege you have of being able to own a copy or even multiple copies of God's love letter to you and to be thankful for the fact that you can read it any time you want to! There are many places in the world where this – still - is not the case.

There are many reliable translations of the Bible available today. I encourage you to find one that is written in a style that you can easily understand and apply. I would then further challenge you to choose a daily Bible reading schedule that allows you to read through the Bible in a year. Don't wait until a new year; start with today's reading and continue until you get back to that same passage. Some things may be harder to understand that way, but it's better than putting it off. (The devil would love for you to totally forget about it.) Pray that God will reveal His Truth to you in a way you can understand and that you can promise to apply to your life. Try to approach His Word with an open, searching heart, without the baggage of things you have heard or have been taught in the past.

The writer of Hebrews assures us, "God's Word is *alive* and *working* and is *sharper* than a double-edged sword. It cuts all the way into us, where the soul and the spirit are joined, to the center of our joints and bones. And it judges the thoughts and feelings in our hearts. Nothing in all the world can be hidden from God. Everything is clear and lies open before Him, and to Him we must explain the way we have lived" (Hebrews 4:12-13).

Everyone is tempted differently, so it definitely does not hurt to also memorize Scriptures that are especially helpful to you (or at least where to find them). They will then more readily come to your mind when you are being tempted. And remember, the Spirit within you can bring those things you have read to your mind when you need them and can provide you the words to speak aloud, if needed.

How does this apply to racism and the battle against it? Remember - your battle is *not* against flesh and blood; therefore, it really has nothing to do with skin tone or nationality or occupation. The devil knows the best strategy to defeat you is to divide and conquer; so if he can use modern technology, media platforms, negative or partial news feeds, current popular beliefs, false religions, or any other number of things to accomplish this task - he will.

Rather than relying on others' opinions – even those of the people closest to you – why not go to the source? God created all things, sees all things, and knows all things; so what better source could we have than His Word?

Years ago, a friend of mine trained to be a bank teller. We had been studying another religious group's beliefs so we could recognize any false teaching. My friend told us that in their training, the tellers *never* studied counterfeits because they were always changing; instead, they studied the *authentic* bills so closely and carefully that they would *always recognize* one that was counterfeit. That's how you need to view God's Word. Get to know it so well that you will recognize when the devil is trying to trick you into believing a counterfeit. I learned a valuable lesson that day and have tried to apply it ever since. In the Bible, God tells us that He is *impartial* in His judgments; He expects the same from you and me.

- THE SHIELD OF RIGHT LIVING

Again, "right living" here uses *God's* standard, **not** man's. What is God's standard? The life and teachings of Jesus and other principles we can find in the Bible – God's inspired word. Many today think that whatever they *feel* - or have been *taught* to believe - is the **right** way to live; but the writer of Proverbs says, "Some people *think* they are doing *right*, but in the end it leads to death." On the other hand, "**Respect** for the Lord gives life. It is like a fountain that can save people from death" (Proverbs 14:12,27). "A truthful witness does not lie, but a false witness tells nothing but lies.... Stay away from fools, because they can't teach you anything.... Fools don't care if they sin, but honest people *work at* being right." This small sampling of truths comes from Proverbs 14, but the whole book of Proverbs is full of priceless wisdom from God and is worth pursuing. Most of the book of Proverbs is attributed to Solomon (the wisest man in history besides Jesus), and it can definitely help us in living right. Since the book of Proverbs has thirty-one chapters and most of our months have thirty or thirty-one days, many have taken the challenge to read one chapter per the corresponding date.

In previous chapters I have touched on the way you are to live, and I will cover how to find and use your unique gifts in a subsequent chapter. But for right now, I want to focus on two main principles:

- **loving God with everything you've got** (which Jesus said was the bottom line to everything, a reference to Deuteronomy 6:5), and

- **loving others as you love yourself - treating others the way you want to be treated:**

putting yourself in others' shoes, so to speak (what many refer to as "The Golden Rule").

The first principle ("Love the Lord your God with all your heart, all your soul, and all your strength.") was to be practiced and taught diligently to your children. If you truly love God, you want to live the way He has taught you - and you want that heritage to continue through your generations. Remember, God has adopted you as His child (if you are a true believer); so He is your Father. Think of how you, as a parent, want your children to live good, fulfilling lives. You give them rules/standards to live by so they can become good citizens and enjoy their lives. Now think about the fact that you are imperfect and don't always know what's best, but God *is* perfect and *always knows* and *wants* the best for you. You will find His guidelines in His Word.

Now think of yourself as a spouse or a friend. You don't want your spouse or friend to ask for a list of what you like and then have him/her check off the list as each task is accomplished. What you *want* is to be known so well that he/she knows what pleases you and does it out of love for you. That's called having a loving *relationship*. God is described in Scripture as a husband to His people. His desire is that you follow His guidelines because you *love* Him and *want* to please Him, not because you are afraid of the consequences if you don't or because you are just checking off a list of do's and don'ts.

The second principle ("Love your neighbor as yourself.") was taken a step further after Jesus washed His disciples' feet. In John 13:34, Jesus gave "a new commandment," which really was an old commandment with new parameters. Instead of just loving others as you love *yourself* (which some of us have a hard time doing), you are now to love others the way *God first loved* you – even if they have hurt you or you think they don't deserve it. As I mentioned before, God's love for you is unconditional. He sent Jesus - His own Son - to be a living example and to die a horrible death, taking on the sins of the whole world - past, present, and future. He was buried and rose again so that *all* of us could *choose* (or not) to accept that gift of perfect relationship with Him forever! *None* of us was, is, or ever will be worthy in and of ourselves.

These principles of right living apply, no matter which side of racism we are on - giving or receiving. As followers of Christ, we *must be living a life of love.*

On the giving end, the way you treat others, regardless of their skin color, race, past, etc. can be a testimony of how Jesus would treat them. We also *teach* our children and others the right way, not only in our words, but also by our examples. Our children are always watching. They see how we treat others (no matter their color, race, or job description) – in our words, expressions, and body language - so we should always be careful to practice what we preach.

On the receiving end of racism, love might appear more like forgiveness. In the book of Acts (Ch. 7), Stephen, a man "full of the Holy Spirit," recounted the Jewish history he shared with his accusers. I can just see them agreeing wholeheartedly with the things he shared about how God had loved and protected them and promised good things for them. But then he called them "stubborn" and "rebellious" because they had not learned the lessons God had shared with their ancestors through the prophets and had not recognized the very One those prophets had promised would come. Stephen went on to accuse these people of killing this One (Jesus), just as their ancestors had killed the prophets sent from God in the past. They responded by stoning Stephen to death. Thus, Stephen became the first Christian martyr; but what impresses me *most* is what he prayed *while* they were stoning him, as recorded in Acts 7:59-60: "'Lord Jesus, receive my spirit.' He fell on his knees and cried in a loud voice, '**Lord, do not hold this sin against them.**' After Stephen said this, he died."

Stephen was a Jew by birth; but because of his faith in Jesus, he was killed. So when I refer to "racism" in this book, I am talking about *anything* that someone may hold against another person *just because* they are a certain gender, race, religion, etc. I am definitely *not* saying that you are likely to die a violent death like Stephen did if someone is prejudiced against you. What I *am* saying is that you can *choose* to **act** or **respond** as Jesus would have you to instead of *reacting* as the devil would want you to react. This can make a tremendous impact on the lives of others – even those who are in the wrong at the time. Case in point: Those people who stoned Stephen laid their coats at the feet of the young man "Saul," who "agreed that the killing of Stephen was good" (Acts 8:1). Saul's name was later changed to Paul. This is the same Paul who made several missionary journeys and established church groups in many different places. Although Saul/Paul was a Jew himself, God **called** him to be an evangelist to the Gentiles. Paul (inspired by the Holy Spirit) wrote many of the letters that we can read in our Bibles today, including the book of Ephesians (the inspiration for *this* book).

What might "right living" look like if someone calls you a name that is offensive in today's culture? Instead of automatically feeling offended or becoming defensive or abusive to that person, perhaps you could give them the benefit of the doubt. Maybe they don't *mean* the term to be offensive at all and just aren't up on the current or local acceptable term. Try educating this person instead of feeling offended all day. If they *are* just mean and hateful, try to imitate Christ by asking yourself how *He* would respond, and act accordingly.

- FOOTWEAR – THE GOOD NEWS OF PEACE

This whole book is based on this item, so I won't go into a lot of detail here; but when you realize that Jesus tore down all physical and spiritual barriers to provide us with salvation, forgiveness, and relationship, you will *want to* share that Good News with everyone else – both in words and in actions. This "footwear" frees you to live a life of true *peace* anywhere and anytime and helps you to "stand strong." The prophet Isaiah put it this way: "How beautiful are the feet of those who bring good news!" (Old Testament quotation found in Romans 10:15 – NIV).

- THE SHIELD OF FAITH

In the NIV, the writer of Ephesians (6:16) tells us to "...take up the shield of faith, with which you can *extinguish* all the flaming arrows of the evil one." Scripture tells us how to get faith, what it is, and what it looks like. I will cover those in this section, but what are "the flaming arrows"? They could include anything that could hurt you or destroy you. They could be racial slurs or even actions against you; so *use* this shield to avoid being hurt, especially in a spiritual sense. Do **not** allow the devil to derail you!

Paul tells us, "So, faith *comes from* hearing the Good News, and people hear the Good News when someone tells them about Christ" (Romans 10:17). The writer of Hebrews shares the *definition* of Biblical faith and more: "Faith means being *sure* of the things we *hope* for and knowing that something is real even if we do not see it. Faith is the *reason* we remember great people who lived in the past. It is *by* faith we *understand* that the whole world was made by God's command so what we see was made by something that cannot be seen" (Hebrews 11:1-3).

The rest of Hebrews 11 shows that faith is an ***active*** word. When each new person is mentioned, his/her name is preceded by "It was by faith…"

and is followed by their obedience to God's command or their belief in the promise given to him/her by God.

Living by faith in God and His Word **protects** your very being. You can see how God has been faithful to His promises all throughout the Bible, and you know how He has been faithful in your own life; so you can have faith that He will continue to keep His promises. You can know that everything will come out all right in the end because He is the righteous judge. You may not *see* the judgment of God in this lifetime, but you can rest assured that He knows all the thoughts and deeds of everyone and that He will judge accordingly. We are not promised that everything will be perfect in this world, but that *even if* the faithful die for their faith, they then will live on with Him for eternity in heavenly perfection!

- THE HELMET OF SALVATION

As humans, our brain is the central part of our bodies; it controls all our other functions. The more we learn about the brain, the more eager we are to protect it with a helmet. Paul tells us to: "Accept God's salvation as your helmet" (Ephesians 6:17a). This gift of salvation protects your soul. I have dealt with this subject fairly extensively, but I will remind you that salvation is a free gift that you could never deserve and that to have it, you must choose to accept it.

On another note, salvation takes away your fear of death; so you can be **confident** and **strong** to live the way you have been called to live, no matter what (I Thessalonians 4:13-5:11).

- THE SWORD OF THE SPIRIT - THE WORD OF GOD

Both "the Belt of Truth" and "the Sword of the Spirit" are referred to as the Word of God. The difference is that one is used in *defense* and the other in *offense*. Your fight is against the devil and his angels (spiritual warfare). **Only** your **spiritual weapon** (the Word of God in the hands of the Spirit we have within us as baptized believers in Christ) is **effective**.

In the Gospel of John (Ch.16), Jesus comforted His disciples, explaining to them that they would be better off after He went back to heaven because then He could send the Helper (His Spirit) to them. The Spirit would **prove** to the world the **truth** about their *sin* (refusing Jesus), about *being right with God* (the Gospel that would be completed when He returned to the Father), and about *judgment* (which He said happened when the ruler of this world was judged). Then Jesus explained to them that He had told them everything they could handle at the time, "But, when the Spirit of Truth comes, He will lead you into all truth" (v. 13). "The Spirit of truth will bring glory to Me, because He will take what I have to say and tell it to you" (v. 14).

What the Holy Spirit brought was God's Word. "*All Scripture* is *inspired by God* and is *useful* for teaching, for showing people what is wrong in their lives, for correcting faults, and for teaching how to live right. Using the Scriptures, the person who serves God will be *capable*, having *all* that is needed to do *every* good work" (II Timothy 3:16-17).

— ❖ —

Paul ends his exhortation to put on the full armor of God by pleading with the Ephesians (and all of us) to **pray** *in* the Spirit – *all* the time and *for everything* and *everyone* (including himself) (Ephesians 6:18-20). So, although prayer is not technically listed as part of the armor of God, it is definitely necessary in our daily lives. Relationship calls for communication. God communicates to us through His Word and His Spirit in various ways; we communicate with Him through prayer.

In this chapter, you've been made aware of what God's armor is - truth, right living, the Good News of peace, faith, and salvation. You need this armor daily, and you must actively put it on in order to "be strong in the Lord and in His great power" (Ephesians 6:10). You know who is your true enemy (the devil) and Who is your great defender (God). You know how to use God's Word for both **offense** (sword of the Spirit) and **defense** (shield of faith).

Now that you know how to defend yourself and are actually equipped to fight the devil, in the next chapter you'll see how you can *taste* the *fruit* that comes from having a relationship with God.

Chapter 7

Taste the Fruit
that Comes from
Relationship with God

M y husband Dewey, a tall man in his early thirties, was sitting in his comfortable, high-backed black leather office chair at his large oak desk in the church study. We had moved to this beautiful town in Northeastern Washington about four years earlier, after living several years in a small desert town in Wyoming.

Dewey had recently started the habit of writing out a Scripture on the back of an old business card and carrying it around unnoticed in his shirt pocket. Several times throughout the day, he would meditate on it and pray for God's guidance to understand its true meaning and significance. When he felt that he understood it better, he would move on to a new verse.

The verse he had chosen this day from his New American Standard version of the Bible was Proverbs 17:16. The passage said, "Why is there a *price* in the hand of the fool to *buy* wisdom when he has no *sense*?" At first, he had chuckled at the pun he heard of "sense" and "cents." He finished copying the verse and put it into his pocket. He had a feeling he might be carrying this one around for a long time before it became clear to him.

He was just about to bow in prayer and then begin meditating on that verse when the sound of the black rotary phone on the corner of his desk jangled, interrupting the quiet. He loved to help people, loved to teach, and loved to talk; so he cheerfully answered the phone.

"Hello, this is Dewey. How may I help you today?"

"Hey, Dewey; this is Sam Johnson," the man answered in an excited tone. "God has brought the most wonderful woman into my life, and I really want you to meet her!"

"What happened to Andrea?" Dewey asked in confusion.

"It's a long story, but Andrea and I have been having problems for a long time. I realize now that I was simply lonely when I met her. I should have waited for God to send me *the one* like when you met Debbie, but I guess I jumped the gun. All of Andrea's nagging and arguing over the past several months have made me so depressed that I nearly gave up on God. But now, God has answered my prayers and sent me my soul mate just when I needed her so desperately. Sally is loving and kind and everything I have always wanted in a woman. She listens to me and needs me, and we both know that God is calling us to be together."

Dewey's heart sank. He and Sam had a history. Sam was sporadic in his church attendance but always very "gung-ho" when he did come. Dewey had hesitated marrying Sam and Andrea a few years prior because Sam had already been married four or five times. Jesus' desire for marriage was one man and one woman for life. Dewey finally had agreed to do the ceremony after giving this couple lengthy premarital counseling and also sharing how God had brought the two of us together from opposite ends of the United States in His own way and timing. (Dewey was from Northwestern Florida, and I was from Southeastern Washington; we both had finally quit trying to find "the one" ourselves.)

Now Sam wanted him to condone a relationship that Dewey knew could *not* be from God. He agreed to meet the couple in an hour's time at the truck stop only a mile from the church office. He ran his fingers through his sandy blond hair and desperately prayed to the Lord to give him the right words to say.

"Father, You *know* that I have given Sam counsel in the past; but it doesn't seem to have done any good. Maybe I'm just not presenting it right. Lord, *please* help me to speak *everything* You want him - and this woman - to hear. Don't allow me to get in the way of your truth. Help me to be confident and not back down just because I may feel uncomfortable."

When he had finished praying, he jotted down a few Scriptures about God's intentions for marriage, about the sins of adultery and fornication, and about testing the spirits to make sure they are sent from God. He prayed again, asking God for a sign that his counsel would be true to God's Word; then he left the safe haven of his office. He felt so vulnerable and helpless.

He arrived at the busy truck stop and found the couple sitting at a booth toward the back on the right. After meeting Sally and hearing them both speak of their certainty that *God* had brought them together, Dewey began sharing the Scriptures proving that it wasn't God, but instead their *own* sinful desires that had sparked this romance. After pouring out his heart and sharing all he could think of, he had the sense that these two *were not* going to listen; they were going to do whatever they *felt* was right.

Just then a tall, stout trucker in a black leather jacket approached their table. Dewey remembered having seen him through his peripheral vision a short time after he himself had arrived, but he hadn't recognized the man and had not even thought about anyone else around their table hearing their conversation.

Making eye contact with the couple, this stranger said, "*Listen* to what this man is saying. He is giving you *wise counsel* and telling you *exactly* what God wants you to hear. Here's one more Scripture for you to consider." He laid a small piece of paper in front of the couple, left to pay his bill, and drove away. Dewey never saw what Scripture was on the paper. (Note: With the exception of Dewey's, names and other details in this example have been changed or omitted to maintain privacy.)

Dewey could hardly wait to get home to tell me how God had answered his prayer so completely. He never saw the stranger again and often wondered if he had been an angel. The incident left Dewey feeling reassured. One thing he knew without a doubt; he had been blessed with a very specific answer to his prayer because of his relationship with God. He also finally understood the Scripture that he'd placed in his pocket that very morning. People may be asking for wise counsel, but if they are not willing to listen and obey God's Word, they are being foolish. *Only* the Spirit of God can convict the world about sin, about being right with God, and about judgment (John 16:7-15).

When I was a teenager, I misunderstood the concept of "bearing fruit" for God. I had lost several young people close to me through car accidents, including the young man I had always assumed I would marry someday. I felt *driven* to share the gospel with others, realizing very early on that life is short and that we don't always have the promise of tomorrow. There was nothing wrong with my *desire* to share, but I would rehearse for hours what the other person might say and how I would respond; I would almost write out a script including verses to answer any question he/she might have in any of these scenarios. If that person did not respond to God's call the way I thought he/she should, I felt like a *failure* to God. God's message is perfect; so in my mind, I must have done or said something wrong. I was relying on *myself,* taking on a burden that God *never* intended me to carry. The fruit of the Spirit is what *God* is doing in *your* life, regardless of what's going on in the lives of others. Remember, it is the Spirit that convicts us and enables us to change. Let the Spirit do His work.

In order for you to enjoy the "fruit [benefits] of the Spirit," you need to understand *what* that fruit is and *where* it comes from. Let's start by asking, where does the fruit of the Spirit come from? Jesus described Himself as "the Vine," His followers as "the branches," and the Father as "the Gardener" Who prunes fruitful branches to produce *more* fruit and also cuts off any unfruitful branches (John Ch. 15). Jesus said, "I Am the Vine, and you are the branches. If any remain in Me and I remain in them, they produce much fruit. But *without* Me they can do *nothing*" (v. 5).

Jesus told us that He gave us an example of how to bear fruit - by remaining in His Father's love and obeying His commands. He told us these things so that we could have *His* joy - "the *fullest possible* joy" (v. 11). Finally, Jesus said, "This is My command: *Love* each other *as* I have loved you.... You are My friends if you do what I command you" (v. 12-14). The fruit of the Spirit begins with love and grows from there.

Paul tells us what the fruit of the Spirit *is* and again says *from Whom* it comes: "The *Spirit* produces the *fruit* of love, joy, peace, patience, kindness, goodness, faithfulness, gentleness, and self-control" (Galatians 5:22-23). Who produces? God's Spirit – *in* you.

Remember, this fruit you enjoy is available to you - *not* because you are educated, smart, talented, famous, rich, male or female, a specific color or race, or because you deserve it or have earned it – but *only* because you have *accepted* a relationship with God and *remain* true to Him. Let's look at each aspect of this fruit of the Spirit:

- LOVE

John tells us more than once that "*God* **IS** *love.*" He tells us how God sent Jesus into this world to show us His love – to die in our place and take away our sins (I John 4:7-21). John says, "This is what *real love* is: It is *not our* love for God; it *is God's* love for us. He sent His Son to die in our place to take away our sins. Dear friends, *if God* loved *us* that much *we also* should love *each other*. No one has ever seen God, but if we love each other, God lives in us, and His love is made perfect in us. We know that we live in God and He lives in us, because He gave us His Spirit" (I John 4:10-13).

The first part of I Corinthians chapter 13 shows that no accomplishment gives us any value or is worth anything if it is not *motivated* by love. Verses 4-8a gives us a picture of what love looks like. I will pass on a challenge given to me in the past. Put *your name* in the place of the word "*love*" (underlined) in this passage: "<u>Love</u> is patient and kind. <u>Love</u> is not jealous, it does not brag, and it is not proud. <u>Love</u> is not rude, is not selfish, and does not get upset with others. <u>Love</u> does not count up wrongs that have been done. <u>Love</u> is not happy with evil but is happy with the truth.

Love patiently accepts all things. It always trusts, always hopes, and always remains strong. Love never ends."

Wow! If you love others this way, think of all the blessings! You will be a better child, sibling, spouse, parent, employee/employer, and friend. Remember, Jesus told you that you are to love your enemies, people who have been unkind to you, and even those who have hurt you to the point of persecution (Matthew Ch. 5). *God's* Spirit *gives* you that *power* to love. This kind of love leaves *no* room for racism or prejudice of *any* kind.

- JOY

I've already mentioned that John tells you Jesus wants you to have *His* joy – the *fullest joy* possible (John 15:11). Two other books in the New Testament immediately come to my mind when I think of joy. The first is Paul's letter to the Philippians, written while he was in prison for sharing the Good News about Christ. The second is the book of James, written by the half-brother of Jesus. Both of these books show that *Biblical joy* is *more than* just "physical" happiness.

Paul describes his situation in prison and other things going on that are outside of his control. Others might have complained, sounding negative and defeated, but not Paul. He *chooses* to be *thankful* and to *have joy* when he remembers his friends in Philippi and is "...always praying with joy for all of you" (Philippians 1:3-4). He says his being in prison has actually *helped* to spread the Good News. Paul knows that some people are trying to upset him by preaching about Jesus for the wrong reasons. But Paul *chooses* to *rejoice* because Christ *is* being preached. He is joyful because of the Philippians' faith and reputation of love. He is joyful to be able to offer himself as a sacrifice for Christ, and he is also joyful for their sacrifice. He tells them to "be full of joy in the Lord" (Philippians

3:1). Paul expresses joy and gratitude that the Philippians are again able to help him in a physical way (Philippians 4:10). Paul goes on to tells us that he has learned the secret to being *content, whatever* the circumstances (Philippians 4:11-12). How? "I can do *all* things *through* Christ, because *He* gives me strength" (Philippians 4:13).

James wrote to Christians who had been scattered because of persecution. He encouraged them to be happy even when they faced troubles and trials, realizing that the *testing* of their *faith* would in turn give them *patience* and that their show of patience would make them **stronger**, giving them ***everything*** they needed (James 1:2-4).

As you can see, the joy Jesus gives you is much deeper than just a bubbly emotion. He gives you the strength and ability to see past your current struggles. Your circumstances no longer rule your thoughts. You can *choose* to be content, knowing that God cares for you and that He is in control.

- PEACE

When I define *peace*, I like to begin by saying what it is *not*. Peace is *not* the absence of conflict; *nor* is it just agreeing with everyone else to avoid conflict, rolling over on your convictions. Jesus describes it this way: "I leave you *My* peace; My peace I *give* you. I do *not* give it to you *as the world* does. So *don't* let your hearts *be troubled* or *afraid*" (John 14:27). He promised that if we love Him and keep His commands, He will ask the Father to send the *Holy Spirit* to *live in* us (John 14:15-19). "I will *not* leave you all alone like orphans; I will *come back* to you.... *Because I live, you will live, too*" (John 14:18-19).

Ephesians 2:11-22 describes Christ's purpose to "make peace" between two groups of people by *taking away* the *hatred* and *uniting* them into *one* group in Him through His own death. Paul actually says, "Christ Himself *is* our peace" (Ephesians 2:14).

Finally, Paul describes why we no longer need to fear death. Jesus has already given us the *victory* over death's power; He has already *paved* the way and *purchased* our ticket to eternity with Him with His own blood. *Death has no more power over us.* We are safe in the arms of Jesus; He has *promised* that when He returns at the end of time, we will be changed into eternal beings and will live with Him forever! That is the ultimate peace (I Corinthians 15:50-58).

- PATIENCE

You may have been warned not to pray for patience because it comes by being faithful through trials; but ultimately, it is still a fruit given by God. What about the patience He has with you? During the first century, non-believers would taunt the Christians of the church because Jesus had not come back yet as He had promised. Some even said that He had *already* come back but that these young Christians had *missed* Him. Peter assures us, "The Lord is *not* slow in doing what He promised – the way some people understand slowness. But God is being *patient* with you. He does *not* want *anyone* to be *lost*, but He *wants all* people to *change* their hearts and lives" (II Peter 3:9).

Look at the patience of Job. Job is the ultimate example of a good person suffering. You can learn a lot from this book. God was proud of Job, but satan told God that the only reason Job obeyed God was because God had given him so much and never let anything bad happen to him; so God first allowed satan to take away *all* Job's *possessions* and *all* his *children*. Job remained faithful; so satan got permission to take away Job's *health*, claiming Job would curse God and die if he was allowed to attack him in that way. Even Job's *wife* turned on him and told him to "curse God and die." "Job answered, 'You are talking like a foolish woman. Should we take only good things from God and not trouble?' In spite of all this Job did not sin in what he said" (Job 2:10).

Next, three of Job's long-time friends came to "comfort" him in his misery; but they ended up making *unfair judgments* against him, thinking he *had to* have sinned in order for all these horrible things to have happened and that *obviously* God was punishing him. But Job refused to make a false confession and to give up on God.

Job finally questioned God, asking, "Why?" and proclaimed his innocence. God answered Job with questions of His own, showing Job that although he wasn't being punished for sin, he still had no right to challenge the Creator. Job responded with humility, admitting that God is all-powerful and that he shouldn't have questioned Him. God then reprimanded the three friends, saying that He'd only forgive them if they made a sacrifice and asked Job to pray for them. They did. After Job prayed for them, God made Job successful again and gave him: *twice* as much as he'd had before, seven more *sons,* three more *daughters* - and he lived to see his great-great-grands.

Job 42:5 sums up Job's experience: "My ears had *heard* of you before, but *now* my eyes *have seen* you." We know from Scripture that no man had actually *seen* God, so Job wasn't speaking in a literal sense here. What he was saying was that before, he knew the things *about* God and how he was to *obey* God; but now he was experiencing "relationship" with God. What a privilege! That's what God offers *you* today.

- KINDNESS

In the last several years there has been a movement called "Random Acts of Kindness." The idea is to do something nice for someone, not expecting anything in return. It is one of the most positive things we have seen people today take hold of, but you know as well as I do that this is not really a new idea at all.

God has shown mankind *His* lovingkindness all throughout history and is recorded in Scripture. Jesus himself told the man who had invited Him to a meal, "When you give a lunch or a dinner, don't invite only your friends, your family, your other relatives and your rich neighbors. At another time they will invite you to eat with them, and you will be repaid. Instead, when you give a feast, invite the poor, the crippled, the lame, and the blind. Then you will be blessed, because they have nothing and cannot pay you back. But you will be repaid when the *good* (NIV says *righteous*) people rise from the dead" (Luke 14:12-14).

I read an anonymous quote the other day that sums up my thoughts on kindness. "Jesus didn't die for us so that we could continue treating people the way people treated Him." Read that again. The people Jesus mentioned in the story from Luke chapter 14 would have been social outcasts - people *different* from His host. With the Spirit's guidance and power, you too can overcome racism and prejudice with kindness.

- GOODNESS

Jesus said, "Only God is good" (Mark 10:18). From its definition, goodness has to do with having high moral standards. Our standards *must* come from God through His written Word (the Bible) and the teachings and example Jesus gave us in Himself.

Paul tells us, "Follow my example, *as* I follow the example of Christ" (I Corinthians 11:1). It's interesting to note that the original documents from which we get today's Bible were not separated into chapters and verses. So, if you look at the few verses directly before this one, you will see that Paul says, "...if you do anything, *do it all for the **glory** of God. Never* do anything that might *hurt others* – Jews, Greeks, or God's church – *just as* I, also, **try** to please *everybody* in *every* way. I am *not* trying to do what is good for *me* but what is *good* for *most people **so*** they can be saved" (I Corinthians 10:31-33). This passage is not saying to change your beliefs, but to try to get along with others – find some common ground so that you can share the Good News with them. Again, it is *God's* Spirit in us that *produces* this "fruit"; and it is powerful.

- FAITHFULNESS

Just as with love, this unwavering *belief* and *confidence* in *God* and *being true* to Him (like an adoring wife to her husband) is based on *God's* being true to love and care for us *first*. All through the Old Testament, we find how God showed His faithfulness to His people; but over and over, they were unfaithful to Him. Especially poignant are the book of Judges and the book of Hosea. The book of Judges repeats a cycle over and over. Everyone did what was right in their own eyes; their enemies would oppress them; they would cry out to God; He would send a judge; they would be faithful until that judge died. Then everything would start over again. Hosea was one of the minor prophets. God had him marry a prostitute who became unfaithful to him. He was instructed to buy her back. God used Hosea's life to show Israel what they had done to Him spiritually and yet how He had kept loving them because of His own faithfulness.

In the New Testament, we are told, "*If we refuse* to accept Him, *He will refuse* to accept us. If *we* are *not* faithful, *He* will *still* be faithful, because He *cannot* be false to Himself" (II Timothy 2:12b-13).

Again, I used to have the wrong definition of faithfulness. I *always rightly* believed that God's love for me was a free gift that could not be purchased, even if I lived a really good life. *But* when I was in the depths of depression for no apparent reason (later I was diagnosed with SADD- Seasonal Affective Depressive Disorder), my husband helped me to understand that my own subconscious *false* belief was getting in the way. I had somehow come to believe that if I could **not** *read* my Bible with understanding, *pray* in complete sentences, or *serve* my family the way I thought I should be able to do, then I was **not** *being faithful* to God.

I was extremely frustrated because I *could not* cope with the everyday responsibilities that I'd been able to fulfill for years (cooking, cleaning, caring for children, etc.). We had prayed that things would return to normal; they did not. I would *try* to read my Bible for comfort and strength, which had always worked in the past; but at this time, I *could not* grasp the meaning – they were just words on a page. I had gotten to the point that I could not complete a full sentence to my husband or even to God. I was so discouraged that I *begged* God to take my life in some way that wasn't my fault (like a plane crash) so that it wouldn't be suicide. That way, I felt assured I would still have a place in heaven.

We'd been studying the book of Revelation; I recognized that the repeated message to the churches was that if they *remained faithful*, they would have an eternity with the Father. Everything would be perfect, no matter how awful it had been for them on earth. Suddenly, I questioned my own place in heaven! What if I were considered *unfaithful* because I couldn't think or function normally?

Dewey came home that day and knelt on the floor by my recliner and asked what he could do to help me.

I burst into tears and desperately answered, "I don't know; that's the problem. I feel like a walking, talking *vegetable*. I want to die so you and the kids will have what you deserve; but for the first time ever, I'm afraid I won't go to heaven because maybe I'm not being faithful!"

He held me in his arms and asked me a series of questions that changed my life and comforted me for years - before the doctors found a medication that worked for me. My depression did not miraculously disappear, but I understood faithfulness better.

"Debbie, do you believe if you could do more for God that He would love you more?"

"No."

"Do you believe He would love you less if you did less?"

"No."

"Do you believe if you were in an accident and became a *vegetable* that God would love you less?"

"Of course not."

"Then why do you think He couldn't love you if you were in fact the *walking, talking vegetable* you've said you feel like?"

"Maybe this is *my* fault? Maybe I've done something that I haven't asked forgiveness for or maybe I haven't lived up to His standards or used my talents to glorify Him." My voice tapered off as I spoke with less conviction.

"Debbie, you *know* that God is faithful; He *knows* what's in your heart. He has heard *all* our prayers; even when you don't know what to say, His Spirit is interceding with groanings too deep for words" (paraphrasing Romans 8:26-27). "God knows your *desires* - you *are* being faithful."

⸻ ❖ ⸻

I shared my struggle with depression because I truly believe God sometimes lets me endure certain things in order to keep me humble and to help others. I also know that the devil wants *you* to feel that you are completely *alone* in whatever struggles *you* are in. But *God is faithful*, and *you are never alone*.

- GENTLENESS

The first thing that comes to my mind when I think of being gentle is what we mothers tell our little children when they encounter helpless babies or little animals. We say, "Be gentle" or "Be soft." Paul told the young Christians of Thessalonica that he and the other apostles had not bribed them, flattered them, or forced them because of their authority when they'd shared the Good News. Instead, they had been "...very gentle with you like a mother caring for her little children" (I Thessalonians 2:7).

The second picture that comes to my mind is of a shepherd carrying a baby lamb back to the flock when it has wandered away. Jesus described Himself as "The Good Shepherd," so you have the perfect example to follow. He is gentle with you, even when you deserve to be disciplined. He loves you that much, and He calls you to treat others the same way.

- SELF-CONTROL

Willpower alone is not enough for you to be able to control yourself. You may have stopped taking drugs or drinking alcohol. You may have lost weight or stayed on a fitness regimen. You may have stopped cursing or gossiping. You may have overcome a lot of faults, but you will never be perfect *except* through the blood of Jesus. Only God's Spirit can help you. If you are relying on yourself, you are fighting a losing battle; you will be miserable. Paul describes this spiritual battle and how blessed we are in the Spirit through Jesus Christ (Romans 7:14-8:17). God's ways are obviously good, but Paul says he finds himself *doing* the wrong things – the very things he hates - and finds himself *not* doing the things he knows he *should* be doing. If he relies on himself, he is completely helpless and overwhelmed. Then he seems to suddenly remember his hope. He says if we belong to Christ, we are set *free* from that old law of sin and death - judged "not guilty." We no longer rely on our sinful selves; instead, we follow the *Spirit's* lead and enjoy *life* and *peace*.

I hope you have begun to taste the fruit of the Spirit – love, joy, peace, patience, kindness, goodness, faithfulness, gentleness, and self-control. Now let's examine how we can experience the joy of relationships with others and embrace our differences.

Chapter 8

Embrace Differences - Experience the Joy of Relationship with Others

My mom's homemade waffles are amazing; so when one of my many nephews told her that he only liked "Portland" waffles, we all laughed, realizing he'd probably only had frozen waffles from the store that you toast in the toaster. Years before that, it was my own kids thinking somebody else's macaroni and cheese didn't taste right because it was homemade or because milk was used when the box recipe called for it; I always seemed to have run out of milk and just used water. The point is that we tend to like what we're used to, and we tend to dislike whatever is different than our norm, even though it may be superior.

The truth is that the world would be a very boring place if we were all the same. Just as children tend to mature and learn to appreciate new or different foods as they grow older, you need to mature and enjoy relationships with people who are different from you. Maybe they are of a different color or race. Maybe they grew up in a totally different environment or even a different country. Maybe they enjoy different types of music, entertainment, or sports. The list of differences could go on forever; but if we *embrace* what makes each of us different, we can enjoy beautiful relationships.

Over the years I've read several inspiring stories on social media. One I particularly remember depicted a white couple who first adopted a couple of black children and then decided to go through an embryo adoption using sperm donated by a black man. The woman successfully carried and birthed triplets. Although some people (both white and black) spoke about and acted towards them in a hateful manner, this couple refused to allow their children or spouse to be abused. They chose to be positive examples of loving - and embracing - the diversity in their family. In another story, a man who chose to adopt a whole family of orphaned children of a different ethnicity led to an entire community being inspired to do what they each could do to make their town a better place.

I'd also like to share insights from some dear friends. (I'll call them John and Mary in order to protect their family's privacy.) Unlike Dewey and myself, John and Mary chose to pursue a private adoption with the assistance of a lawyer and a doctor. Like us, they too had to endure the unfathomable pain of having a birth mother change her mind and having to give up the child they had anticipated for so many months. Mary said it nearly broke her heart in two. If she hadn't had the support of a dear Christian sister who prayed and cried with her for hours, she doesn't think she could have gone on.

Sometime later, they tried again. Mary said the birth mother was white, but the little boy born to her was obviously black. She said it didn't matter what color he was; he was their son! Later, they added a baby girl to their lovely family. Again, the birth mother was white; but the baby was black. Mary and John didn't care what color their children were and didn't try to indoctrinate these children in any particular culture.

When I talked with Mary, I asked if they or their kids had been treated differently because of their color. She told me she didn't think so. She said, "To us, they weren't white or black; they were simply *our kids*. We raised them just like anyone else would raise their own children. I would say more people probably questioned us about why we adopted than they did about the color of their skin."

I was not around when these two children were adopted or when they were growing up, but I did get to meet the girl one year at teen camp where I was cabin counselor. I was deeply impressed with this beautiful young lady - with the kindness and compassion she showed towards all the other campers and with how polite she was to all the adults. Later, I was proud to hear how she had gone on to play college basketball and that she was still a truly amazing, humble young lady. Both she and her brother are now adults and are living happy, productive lives. I haven't seen the young man for many years, but I recently got to see the young lady. She is happily married to a white man and works for a college remotely; she and her husband recently welcomed their second child. Their toddler is adorable, both in looks and personality; the grandparents couldn't be more proud.

I've shared examples of parent/child and adoption relationships, but what about diversity in a marriage relationship? First of all, God created men and women to each have different strengths and different needs so they could be perfect helpmates to one another. It was "not good for man to be alone," so God created woman. In a good marriage, a husband and wife complete each other. That's *not* to say they are exactly alike. Hence the saying, "Men are from Mars; Women are from Venus." It seems we are different enough to be from different planets!

In many ways, my husband Dewey and I were opposites. Dewey grew up in hot and humid Florida, just outside a large city; I grew up in dry, sunny Eastern Washington in a small rural town. He was the fourth of five children born to older parents; I was the first of five children born to very young parents. He was a spender; I was a saver. He liked to go places and be busy; I often preferred to stay home and read a book. He seemed to notice very minute details in seconds; I never seemed to focus on details unless they were pointed out to me. Dewey liked to talk; I preferred to listen. He was very creative; I was not. He was very mechanically inclined and seemed to be able to fix anything; I knew "righty-tighty, lefty-loosey" and could name a few basic tools. Dewey liked to lead; I liked to follow. Dewey had a good voice and sang, but music didn't' seem to impact him much; I have always loved to sing and perform because music touches me deeply. Dewey had determined to stop talking if ever he felt he was starting to get angry; I wanted to hash it out and get it over with, "not letting the sun go down on my anger." Dewey wanted to talk about important things deep into the night; I fell asleep as soon as my head hit the pillow.

Again, the list could go on; but those differences didn't matter because we were both united in love and purpose. We used our differences to help keep the other in check and to serve one another. For instance, sometimes I would ask Dewey what a new piece of equipment or vehicle he wanted would do that the one we already had wouldn't do; so I helped keep his spending in check. Dewey would sometimes come with me to perform at a local country jam session so that I could enjoy his company and sing harmony instead of the lead. He didn't really enjoy this the way I did. It was outside his comfort zone, but he did it especially for me. We learned to compromise, and each of us was committed to giving 100% in our relationship. We were able to live in harmony because we were united on the important things. We both loved God first and foremost, and we *chose* to work through any differences of opinion we might have. We always tried to build each other up in love, both when we were together and when we talked about one another to others.

⸺◇◆◇⸺

I always like to hear other people's love stories; so I will share mine. Dewey and I met in Texas, where he and my brother attended preaching school. I had flown down from Seattle to visit my brother and sister-in-law for the Christmas holidays. I needed to get away from the physical side of a relationship I was in so that I could reason with my heart and mind instead of my desires and to decide rationally if I should let the relationship continue or to break it off. I had come close to eloping with my boyfriend, but something held me back; it wasn't because he was Hispanic or even that he was a recovering alcoholic. I just really felt I needed to marry a strong, mature Christian man who would be the *leader* of our family. Most of the guys I'd dated (including this current one) were newer to the faith. It seemed to me that the more established Christian men were either already married or simply were not interested in me as anything more than a sister in Christ. I was finding it hard to wait for the Lord's timing, and I agonized over the idea that I was destined to be "an old maid." I was only twenty-three, but my mom had married at fifteen and already had three kids (the youngest of whom was three) by the time she was my age.

My brother and sister-in-law had told me about a couple of single guys at the preaching school they thought I might be interested in, but I didn't dream I would find "the one" or that any of those guys would be interested in me. I even told them not to set me up on a blind date and to convey that if we did go out, it would just be as friends because I hadn't broken up with my boyfriend. I didn't really believe in love at first sight; so although I thought Dewey was very attractive, I didn't actually begin falling in love with him the first time I *saw* him - but I *did* when we *talked*. We didn't talk about sports or the weather. He began talking about life goals and what he thought was most important in life. He believed a preacher had to be careful to put his family before his job, even though God had to remain number one on the throne of his life.

I was amazed to find that there was actually a *single* man who had the same ideals I had – and since he had spoken of them first, I was *sure* that he wasn't just agreeing with me to impress me. In case he'd had that same thing happen to him, I made sure to share some not-so-popular views myself, and he agreed with me! I didn't find out until years later that Dewey had basically begun to believe that all women were the same - they just wanted to marry a man who would become a doctor or a lawyer and make lots of money. He was trying to speed up the inevitable by "cutting to the chase" so that he could forget all about me and go to see his family for

Christmas Break after he finished his finals. After our conversation, he had to admit to himself that maybe he had been mistaken about *all* women being the same.

I knew after that first conversation; I would have to break up with my boyfriend back home as soon as I got back, even if Dewey wasn't interested in me romantically. I finally realized not only was God capable of preparing someone special for me, but He had already done so. I would be patient instead of *settling* for less. My biggest worry at that point was how I would explain to the guy back home that he wasn't the one for me without making him feel bad. I worried that he would not yet be strong enough in his new-found faith to remain faithful to Christ without my encouragement.

After my enlightening conversation with Dewey, I asked my brother to invite him over for dinner that night. I cooked my special homemade enchiladas for him. While I was finishing up in the kitchen, I got a phone call from my dad letting me know my boyfriend had *not* left my car at my house after driving me to the airport, as I had told my parents he would. Dad thought perhaps the guy had misunderstood my directions; but since we'd had an argument about why I'd allow my *parents* to borrow my car while theirs was in the shop instead of lending it to *him* for two weeks, I knew it wasn't an accident. I didn't know if or when he would return my car; but at that point, I remember feeling *relieved* that I wouldn't have to worry about how he reacted to my breaking up with him. Dewey, having been warned by my sister-in-law that I might be upset when I returned to the living room, was surprised that I didn't seem upset at all (and now *you* know why).

That was Tuesday night. I saw Dewey again on Thursday and went out to lunch with him. We then went to a gathering of preacher students and their families later that night where Dewey had agreed to play Santa. On the way back, we got lost on the freeway because of all the loops, but we finally made it back to my brother's house. We sat in Dewey's truck late into the night talking, during which time he invited me to join him the next day on his drive to Florida to spend Christmas with his family after finishing his finals. I didn't want to be an encroachment on his time with his mom, especially since he'd missed the previous Christmas holiday to spend time with a previous girlfriend's family; and besides, I was *supposed* to spend the holiday with my brother and sister-in-law. However, when my sister-in-law heard about his invitation, she insisted I should say yes if he asked again. So when he called Friday morning to say his mom *wanted* me to come and that he'd already made all the arrangements, I agreed to go.

Just as we got out of the big city, Dewey's truck tire went flat. I remember thinking it was ironic because we had gotten lost the night before, but I was impressed by his calm demeanor and his efficiency in changing the tire. We arrived in Florida, and I loved his whole family; by the end of my two-week vacation, we were "unofficially" engaged. (Dewey said it wouldn't be "official" until he had asked for my dad's permission to marry me - in person.)

I did **not** get my car back right away after returning home to Seattle. I worked in a town north of Seattle to which there was no bus service; so I used my parents' car and stayed with them for a while since they were living close by at the time. Dewey and I communicated through letters and phone calls; he even sent me an audio tape of himself singing some country songs, which I would play as I cleaned. (I worked as a nanny/housekeeper at that time.) The little two-year-old girl to whom I was nanny would reach for the tape first thing when I arrived, saying, "*My* Dewey! *My* Dewey!"

My parents and I were able to attend my brother's and Dewey's graduation from preacher's school in late January, and then we flew back home. Dewey, in the meantime, helped my brother and sister-in-law move back up to Washington State from Texas. My dad was really nervous about Dewey "officially" asking to marry me; so he suggested Dewey send a note with a box on which he could check yes or no, but that didn't fly. When Dewey got to Washington and asked for my hand, not only did my dad give us his blessing (after making sure that Dewey and I had the same ideals of marriage), but he also suggested we not continue to have a long distance romance, racking up phone bills until marrying in April or May as we had planned. He instead suggested we get married while Dewey was in Seattle that first week of February before he was to report to his new job in Upstate New York. So we did! It was a whirlwind of activity, but we made it.

We purchased the marriage license, bought Dewey's white pants and shoes to go with the navy blue double-breasted blazer he had with him, and bought rings for both of us. I had already ordered my dress from a JC Penny catalog (since my dad had told me he'd say yes when Dewey asked him). I figured ordering the dress early would give me time to make any adjustments by April or May, but the Victorian-style dress *actually* fit me perfectly when it arrived in time for our now February wedding. All I had left was to purchase white shoes.

My brother performed the wedding ceremony in the fellowship hall at the church I'd attended while living in Seattle. A day before we were married, I actually got to have a "candle passing" (Sunday night after church). A "candle passing" was a tradition I was introduced to at the

Christian college I'd attended years before. The newly engaged woman would blow out the candle holding her engagement ring after it had been passed around and admired. I had wanted a candle passing of my own ever since. Several women in the congregation had attended that same college and were familiar with the tradition, but I knew *nobody* would guess it was me who was engaged (except for my roommates, in whom I'd already confided). They had only just met Dewey at church service that very morning, and most knew nothing about how my ex-boyfriend had stolen my car or that we had broken up. The candle passing also gave me the opportunity to invite several of my church friends to the wedding that would be held the following night.

On my wedding day, one of my roommates purchased a wedding cake and a bouquet of flowers at Albertsons and then brought them by a Metro bus (her normal mode of transportation) to the church building. My mom is still impressed with that fact to this day. Several friends from church who'd been downstairs practicing songs for worship came upstairs and sang the song, "Bind Us Together" as I requested. My roommate stood up as my maid of honor, and the two of us sang a favorite secular song of ours during the ceremony. Another friend took a video of the ceremony and reception and gave it to us as a wedding gift. All in all, it turned out to be the beautiful church wedding of my dreams with very little expense and without having all the time to fret and worry about details. Our only regret was that nobody from Dewey's family was able to attend at such short notice. For several years, Dewey thought he'd like for us to renew our vows so that more family members could attend; but after performing several marriage ceremonies himself over the years and seeing all the glitches and worries in even the best planned services, he came to the conclusion that he was pretty happy with our wedding ceremony just as it was.

Our first home together was in Upstate New York, where Dewey had lived for a few years before attending preaching school in Texas. I soon learned to embrace not only *our* differences, but also the differences in others around us. I had never lived anywhere except the Northwest; the Northeast was a bit of a culture shock for me.

I remember walking down the sidewalk with Dewey one morning after only being in New York for a few weeks. I smiled and waved at a man walking toward us. Where I grew up, that was the polite and friendly thing to do; but this man looked at me warily as though he thought I was going to try to steal something from him. I asked Dewey what I'd done wrong. He answered with a smile, saying that people on the East Coast weren't *unfriendly;* they were just more cautious and private than people down South or from the West Coast. He explained that if you walked down the street where *he* grew up down South, everyone would smile and wave and *seem* to be friendly; but although people in Upstate New York might not be so open at first, when they *did* warm up to you, they would be true friends *for life*. He went on to tell me that one time his truck broke down when he'd lived there before, and several guys from his church *volunteered* to take time off work to help him fix it! He couldn't imagine his friends down South doing something like that for anyone. (He warned me, though, that New Yorkers were still very *private;* so I was *never* to ask how much someone paid for something because that would be deeply offensive to them.) In the eight months we lived there, I learned to love the people deeply - differences and all.

What does God and His Word have to say about relationships with others who are different from you? I've already shared from the Gospels about loving your enemies and praying for those who persecute you - and from Galatians, Ephesians, and others about family relationships; but in the book of Romans, we're also told about other people we are to love.

In the book of Romans, Paul addressed both Jews and Gentiles, telling them God had used the Gentiles to make the Jews jealous so that they would return to relationship with Him, and also warning the Gentiles that if they became arrogant, they would lose their new-found relationship. The solution was for the Jews and Gentiles to love one another and to pray for each other; *all* were to rely on God's bountiful mercy (Romans Ch. 11).

Paul said to them, "So brothers and sisters, since God has shown us great mercy, I beg you to offer your lives as a living sacrifice to Him. Your offering must be only for God and pleasing to Him, which is the spiritual way for you to worship. Do not change yourselves to be like the people of this world, but be changed within by a new way of thinking. Then you will be able to decide what God wants for you; you will know what is good and pleasing to Him and what is perfect" (Romans 12:1-2).

The advice Paul gives the Romans extends to us also. He tells us not to think too highly of ourselves, but to use our gifts to serve each other with a genuine love. We are to be empathetic and to live in peace. We are to be humble enough to befriend those who *seem* unimportant. Paul said that some were weak and some were strong; in relation to special days and whether or not to eat certain foods, we were all to stand by our *own* convictions. *None* of us is to *judge* another, to think ourselves better than others, to *force* our own opinions on others, *or* to make them stumble because of our own

freedom (Romans Ch. 14).

Paul says (Romans Ch. 15) that the strong are not to just please themselves, but to follow Christ's example by thinking of the good of others and helping the weak to become stronger in faith. He further tells us that "Everything that was written in the past was written to teach us. The Scriptures give us patience and encouragement so we can have hope. Patience and encouragement come from God. And I pray that God will help you *all agree with each other* (NIV says *have a spirit of unity*) the way Christ Jesus wants. Then you will all be *joined together* (NIV says *unified)*, and you will give glory to God the Father of our Lord Jesus Christ. Christ accepted you, so you should accept each other, which will bring glory to God" (Romans 15:4-7).

In this chapter, we've seen through both example and Scripture that we are to love and respect one another, embracing our differences, using them as checks and balances and in service to one another. We can see through Scripture that Jesus is the answer to the problem of racism and prejudice in *any* form. He has broken down **all** the walls. Why would we try to rebuild them?

You can use **your** gifts to build up and encourage others in love just as Maggie and her family were able to do in the dream story I shared with you in chapter one. In the next chapter, we will discuss how you can *find* your unique gifts and how to *use* them to combat racism.

Chapter 9

Find Your Unique Gifts to Combat Racism

"Why did I not have the gifts the wife of one of our elders had?" I wondered. She always seemed to know when to make a dinner and take it to people just when they needed it, whether it was for our family as we moved into our new house or after we'd been out cutting wood all day - or for others when they were sick or just out of the hospital. She organized and cleaned at the church building as if it were her own home. Her own house was always clean and ready for unexpected company. The other elder's wife was always offering to take care of our kids so we could have a Sunday afternoon nap - after she'd already helped me with them all through the church service. She also seemed to know everyone in town and was always on top of everything, meeting the needs of others in her own way. I was appreciative of their gracious acts of service to others, but somehow I felt inadequate.

Here I was the preacher's wife. Wasn't I supposed to be doing all those things? Why hadn't God given me *those* gifts? I had been diagnosed with SADD (Seasonal Affected Depressive Disorder) a few years prior; I wasn't able to be consistent with housekeeping or with disciplining the kids. I was so overwhelmed just trying to keep up with my everyday responsibilities that I had no energy to even think about how to meet the needs of others. When we'd moved to this town for Dewey's new preaching position, we had four young children - the boys in 3rd and 1st grades and the twin girls almost three. As I think I've already mentioned, I'm not very observant; I never seem to know what's going on outside my own little world. The only things I felt I'd been gifted with were taking care of little children (except of course in the winter when the SADD kicked in) and singing. How was I supposed to help my husband meet the needs of this new congregation when I was such a mess?

―◈―

Have you ever felt that you just don't have what it takes to be an effective servant of God? Have you ever *not* felt that way? I struggled for years with SADD; without proper medication, it was getting worse every year. Eventually I only felt good in late spring and early summer, which meant that I really was only at my norm for two or three months out of the whole year. It took fifteen years for me to find a medication that worked for my body, allowing me to return to *my* normal year-round. By that time, our children were mostly grown, at least past their most formative years. I felt I had failed them as a parent for never having been able to be consistent with guidelines and discipline or to have been an example as a servant to others.

About ten years before Dewey died, he found a real treasure at a thrift shop for only a quarter. He wasn't an avid reader (except for the Bible), but he felt called to read this book by Wayne Cordeiro called The Divine

Mentor. We both ended up reading it, and it changed our lives by changing the way we read the Bible and how we thought of the people in the Bible as real "mentors" instead of just "characters." It taught us to appreciate the *privilege* of reading God's Word even more than we had before. We bought several copies and passed them around to members of our congregation and other friends and family. Dewey encouraged church members to follow the Bible reading schedule included in the book. We then each taught our separate classes, and he also preached from something we *all* had read that week.

During this time, we held a class on Wednesday nights; several of us would take turns sharing a Scripture that had really touched us during the previous week. I already knew that God is the one who gives us gifts and that not everyone has the same gifts, but I finally realized (in rereading I Corinthians Ch. 12) that His **Spirit** is responsible for who gets what - and where we are placed. So that meant I had the gifts God wanted me to have in the place where God wanted me to be. One fellow-believer helped to forever solidify this fact in my mind by telling me that if I were not thankful for what God had given me and instead thought I should have somebody else's gifts, I actually would be saying that I knew better than God and that He didn't know what He was doing. Yikes! That certainly got my attention and made me think twice. That is not to say that I shouldn't seek more gifts - especially faith, hope, and love - but that I shouldn't "covet" someone else's gifts (I Corinthians 12:31-14:1 and 14:12).

God created you to be a unique individual with talents, abilities, and thoughts completely your own. He also created you to work together with others in unity and harmony just as your individual body *parts* work together for the good of your *whole* body (I Corinthians 12; Romans 12:3-8).

It is not a competition. As Christians, we are not trying to get the glory for ourselves; we are all on the same team, working together to build up the body of Christ (His church) and to help others find the wonderful free gifts He offers.

How do you know what your gifts are? Think of the things you are especially good at doing or things that you are especially interested in. You can begin there, using those to bring honor and glory to God. Jesus told a parable about a master leaving differing amounts of money with three of his servants to take care of while he was on a journey. When he returned, the first and second servants were praised for doubling the master's money; they were given more responsibilities and rewards as a result. The third servant was condemned. Because he was afraid, he had simply buried the money while his master was away and then gave it back to the master when he returned. That with which he had been entrusted was taken away and given to the first servant. The parable was regarding money, but the principle involves our talents/gifts. If you don't use them, you lose them; use them, and you gain more (Matthew 25:14-30 and Luke 19:11-27).

What if you *still* don't know what gifts you have? First, you should **pray** about it. **Ask God** to reveal to you what your gifts are. He *wants* you to come to Him as a child would to a parent. He *wants* to give you good gifts. He may show you through Scripture or He may use one or more of His people. He may even show you through some crisis or circumstance. Many of us have been taught to be humble; we find it hard to identify ways in which we stand out. **Ask people** who know you what it is about you that stands out to them – what makes you unique or special to them. **Think** about the qualities you needed to possess in order for you to do the job you have chosen. Finally, **rely** on His **Spirit** to guide you into *using* your gifts to God's glory. As Paul says, "*Everything* you do or say should be done to obey Jesus your Lord. And in *all* you do, give thanks to God, the Father through Jesus" (Colossians 3:17).

If you are just now starting to *recognize* your gifts, **when** can you use them and **what** do you do with them, specifically in regards to racism? Like so many other things I've talked about, there is *no end* to the possibilities. For instance, let's say you have a real gift of encouragement. From the time you get up in the morning, you can encourage your family with a smile and with encouraging words and service. You can influence them and others with whom you come in contact during your day by your example. Take the time to thank people who are simply doing their jobs. You will be surprised at how easily you can honestly compliment the clerk at the grocery store, the janitor at the school, or even someone walking down the street. Your encouragement can totally change their demeanor and possibly even their outlook on life. Don't limit yourself to only people who are in the same line of work as you or who are the same color, race, or religion as you are. Be an encourager to *all*.

Be generous with your gifts, no matter what they are. As you use your gifts, you will find yourself becoming better at them - and you will also gain more gifts. You will find that you can *never* out-give God. Jesus said, "Give, and you will receive. You will be given muCh. Pressed down, shaken together, and running over; it will spill into your lap. The way you give to others is the way God will give to you" (Luke 6:38).

The previous few paragraphs show ways you can use your gifts as an *individual*. You can also find a *group* in your church or community where you can use your gifts in service to others. When you combine your talents with those of others, you can accomplish even greater things. Maybe your talent is coming up with creative ideas or organizing events. If so, maybe you could take the *lead* in a service project. Gather a group of others (like me) who do not share those particular talents, but who really want to *help* serve. If you are more of a follower (like me), look for a group already serving in some way and volunteer (city cleanup projects, soup kitchens, helping the elderly with yard work, etc.).

Paul talks about the church working together as the body of Christ. He says that we may come from different walks of life and have different talents or functions; but even if we don't *think* we are an important part, it doesn't make us any *less* a part of the body. "The foot might say, 'Because I am not a hand, I am not part of the body.' But *saying* this would *not* stop the foot from *being* a part of the body." Paul also points out that one body part can't say to another, "I don't need you!" "...But God put the body together and gave more honor to the parts that need it *so* our body would *not be divided*. God wanted the different parts to care the same for each other." If one part suffers, all suffer; if one part is honored, all share in that honor (I Corinthians Ch. 12; quoted vs. 15, 24-25).

Think about your physical body. Every part has a purpose and function. You may not realize the importance of your little finger. But my late husband could attest to the fact that *if* it were missing, you would have to learn to compensate for things you may have always taken for granted. When he cut off his little finger in a table saw accident, the immediate reaction was that his whole body suffered. He guarded his right hand with his left. He showed signs of shock. After surgery, his head ached and his stomach churned; he couldn't control the pain and nausea. When he woke up from surgery, the doctor told him the little finger was *not* important and that he'd *never* miss it; he had removed it instead of restoring it. Wrong!

Dewey said that not only did he have phantom pain and itching, but he also had to learn to twist his wrist in order to even hold a bar of soap or to catch the coins the clerk gave him as change at the store. He had to resort to more of a "hunt and peck" method of typing. He had to do a lot of hand exercises in order to just be able to hold and use tools again, and it took *years* to regain his grip strength.

So, to recap, you need to *recognize* the talents God has chosen to give you and to *use* them to *His* glory. You should remain humble, but not be self-deprecating. Work together *with* others to promote the good *in* others and *for* others. Use your talents to *build up,* not to tear down.

To illustrate how God can use one person's talents to encourage another who doesn't feel qualified to accomplish the task he has been asked to do, I want to share another story from Dewey's past. The church had asked him to lead the teen class, as opposed to the adult class with which he was much more comfortable and confident. Dewey had been very shy as a teen, and our own children were still very young. He felt very unqualified, but he did as he was asked and used his teaching skills to the best of his ability. One weekday morning after having taught this class for several months, he was feeling exceptionally inept; he prayed to God about three *specific* areas in which he felt especially inadequate, begging for God's help and guidance to get through to these teens. He was convinced that he was making no difference at all in their lives.

Dewey came home from his church office across the parking lot, checking and reading the mail on his way in for lunch. He could hardly believe the way God answered his prayer, spoken only an hour before. God used the gifts of encouragement and writing in one of the teen girls from his class to send an encouraging letter to Dewey, addressing *all* three of those specific things about which he had prayed. This letter *had* to have been written and sent at least two days *prior to* his praying that prayer in order for him to receive it that day. This particular young lady rarely spoke up in class; Dewey had never seen a sample of her writing, so to hear from her in this way was *totally* unexpected. This was completely what I have come to call "a *God* thing" (or instead of coincidence, a *God*-incidence).

Can God accomplish His work in spite of the odds? Oh, yes, He can – and He does!

The devil (and the world he influences) wants you to *bury* your talents and to *give in* to hate, evil, revenge, and racism; but God encourages you through the apostle Paul to *not* be lazy, to *use* your gifts with a good attitude and wholeheartedly. It's a little lengthy, but I want to share the short, meaty statements given in Romans 12:9-21:

"Your love must be real. Hate what is evil, and hold on to what is good. Love each other *like brothers and sisters* (NIV says *in brotherly love*). Give each other more honor than you want for yourselves. Do not be lazy but work hard, serving the Lord with all your heart. Be joyful because you have hope. Be patient when trouble comes, and pray at all times. Share with God's people who need help. *Bring strangers in need into your homes* (NIV says *Practice hospitality*).

Wish good for those who harm you; wish them well and do not curse them. Be happy for those who are happy and be sad with those who are sad. Live in peace with each other. Do not be proud, but make friends with those who seem unimportant. Do not think how smart you are.

If someone does wrong to you, do not pay him back by doing wrong to him. *Try to do what everyone thinks is right* (NIV says *Be careful to do what is right in the eyes of everyone*). Do your best to live in peace with everyone. My friends, do not try to punish others when they wrong you, but wait for God to punish those who do wrong; 'I will repay them,' says the Lord. But you should do this: 'If your enemy is hungry, feed him; if he is thirsty, give him a drink. Doing this will be like pouring burning coals on his head' (quoted from Proverbs 25:21-22). Do not let evil defeat you, but defeat evil by doing good."

I have shared ways in which you can identify your unique gifts and have given a few examples of how you might choose to use those gifts in service to others. We have learned the importance of *using* the gifts with which God has blessed us to avoid losing them. We have also learned that using our gifts to benefit *all* people (as opposed to others just like ourselves) can help in reducing racism and prejudice.

I have one more promise to fulfill. In the next - and last - chapter, I would like to share how *you* can become the change that impacts millions and make a difference in this racist world, *even if* you are not a well-known person, a political figure - or even politically-minded at all.

Chapter 10

Become the Change – You Can Impact Millions

One of my fondest high school memories is of meeting a girl who came to class as a new student. I was immediately drawn to her. Although we didn't have all our classes together, we spent every possible moment getting to know one another that first day she came to school. We kept discovering similarities in values, likes and dislikes, and other such things; we both went home to tell our moms about this girl we'd met at school. The next day she came to school saying, "Guess what, Debbie! We're cousins!"

Her mom had recognized my last name (also her maiden name), and she knew my parents. It turns out this new girl and I had grandfathers who were brothers, yet here we grew up in towns close to each other and never even knew the other existed. We lost touch for quite a while after high school, but we reconnected several years ago. Dewey and I were able to celebrate our thirtieth and most memorable anniversary in Alaska, spending part of that trip with this special cousin and her family fishing and catching up on old times. I still count this cousin as a dear, close friend.

❖

One of my brothers recently started a simple family tree so that our generation could recognize at least the *names* of some of the cousins we don't even know about and *how* we're related. Our dad is the youngest of thirteen children. His mom and dad (my grandparents) are the beginning of this particular tree; as you can imagine, it is huge. My brother is finding it difficult to display the tree so that it can be seen altogether. Extended family (and our mom) have provided valuable information to fill in gaps on the families he doesn't know.

Many people don't have such a big family, but I have been noticing lately that friends will post past pictures of themselves with their spouse and children. Then they post a picture of how their family has grown to include their children's spouses and families and sometimes also their grandchildren's families - until it looks like everyone can hardly fit in the picture. This growth pattern is one way you change the world.

❖

So what does all this family tree business have to do with our impact on others? Quite a lot, actually. I am not a political figure, nor do I consider myself a major player in the places I've lived. Since I am not well known and my sphere of influence is small, how is it that I can impact millions?

109

Discipleship. In a family tree, it starts with two people and multiplies throughout the generations. My cousin and I had similar values that were shown and taught to us by our parents and grandparents. As a mom, I have an influence on my children by the example and teachings I gave and continue to give; they, in turn, can pass these values to the next generation, and so on.

This principle is not new. Moses said, "Listen, people of Israel! The Lord our God is the only Lord. Love the Lord your God with all your heart, all your soul, and all your strength. Always remember these commands I give you today. Teach them to your children, and talk about them when you sit at home and walk along the road, when you lie down and when you get up. Write them down and tie them to your hands as a sign. Tie them on your forehead to remind you, and write them on your doors and gates" (Deuteronomy 6:4-9).

Teaching and leading your own family by example may be a start, but what if you aren't married or don't have children? Jesus was not married, yet He made the *greatest* impact of anyone on earth - for *all* generations. *How*? He gave us an example of *discipleship* and taught us that if we have faith even the size of a mustard seed, we can move mountains. Both in family and in other relationships of discipleship, the starting point is small but the end is exponential.

Jesus knew what His mission was and that He had very little time in this world in which to accomplish it. His earthly ministry was only three years in length and ended with His death, burial, and resurrection; yet by God's power, His *impact* on this world is still felt today. Jesus began teaching and healing people publicly only after He had prepared Himself. That preparation included His baptism, a period of prayer and fasting, and undergoing an intense time of temptation in the wilderness. He would often go off to a lonely place to spend time alone with His Father (Luke 4:42, 5:16). We learn of one specific time in which Jesus spent all night in prayer on a mountain and then chose twelve of His disciples (followers) to be named apostles (messengers) (Luke 6:12-16).

These twelve men would live, travel, and work with Jesus for approximately three years as they learned from Him. Jesus chose an eclectic group. Some were fishermen by trade; He told them they would now "fish for people" (Mark 1:17). Others included men who would have been sworn enemies of each other - for instance, Simon the Zealot and Levi (Matthew) the tax-collector. A Zealot would have strictly adhered to Jewish Law; a tax-collector (employed by the Roman government) was considered a traitor by the Jews. Jesus, fully knowing that Judas Iscariot would later betray Him, called even Judas to be one of these twelve. Jesus knew what was in the heart of each of these men. He gave them *all* a perfect example and taught them constantly.

On the night Jesus was betrayed, *none* of those closest to Him could even *guess* who the betrayer would be. Jesus was not unkind in the way He spoke to Judas or in the way He treated him (even when He washed the apostles' feet). His example shows us how we, too, are to always be kind and loving to those around us, even if we suspect ulterior motives.

Of the twelve men Jesus chose, three seem to have been closer to Jesus or at least to have had some unique experiences the larger group did not have. Only Peter, James, and John were invited into the room when Jesus raised Jairus' daughter from the dead (Mark 5:21-43). Jesus also took Peter, James, and John up on a high mountain where He was "changed" and spoke to Moses and Elijah (Matthew 17:1-13; Mark 9:2-13; Luke 9:28-36).

A third experience that only these three disciples shared with Jesus was when He went away from the others to pray in the Garden of Gethsemane on the night He was betrayed (Matthew 26:36-46 and Mark 14:32-42).

Of those three men, John (brother of James and son of Zebedee) refers to himself in his own gospel account as "the follower Jesus loved." It was also John whom Jesus chose to take care of His mother after His death on the cross (John 19:25-27 and 21:20-25).

Why bring up these things? Because - just like Jesus, *you* have a sphere of influence. Some people may only be acquaintances or even friends of friends – some encounters may be very brief, without even an exchange of names. Others may be like the women who followed Jesus and physically helped sponsor and care for Him and His disciples from their own means – sometimes from afar. As the circle narrows, you have your close family and/or friends with whom you have a more constant and quality connection. Then you have those two or three friends with whom you feel the most comfortable and share with on a much more intimate level. You may even have that *best* friend in whom you can entrust your own life and those of your loved ones. My best friend was my husband – my soul mate; but God is able to fill that physical gap in my life with special friends who disciple me or whom I can disciple – and He will do the same for you. Unlike Jesus, you do *not* know the hearts and minds of those around you. You are not to judge motives, but you must realize that even if you show and teach others the high standards of Jesus (discipling), *some*, like Judas, will choose *not* to embrace those values. Do **not** give up if some choose not to follow Jesus, even if they are your own family members.

Scripture doesn't tell us exactly what happened in the lives of each of Jesus' twelve apostles, but we are told that Judas betrayed Jesus and that the rest of the disciples were scattered when Jesus was arrested – as the prophets had written (Matthew 26:47-56 and John 16:32-33). We also learn that Judas tried to right his wrong by returning the betrayal money, but the Jewish leaders would not accept it - so Judas threw the money into the Temple and went out and hanged himself (Matthew 27:1-10; prophecies fulfilled: Zechariah 11:12-13 and Jeremiah 32:6-9). We know that Peter denied knowing Jesus three times (just as Jesus had said he would), but that he wept when he realized his failure to be faithful and then relied on the mercy and forgiveness Jesus offered instead of relying on himself (Matthew 26:31-35,69-75; Mark 14:66-72; Luke 22:31-34,54-62; John 18:4-11; 20:3-9; 21:7,15-25).

We also know that Jesus gave final instructions to the remaining eleven chosen disciples after He rose from the dead. Jesus told them, "All power in heaven and on earth is given to Me. So go and make followers (disciples) of all people in the world. Baptize them in the name of the Father and the Son and the Holy Spirit. Teach them to obey everything that I have taught to you, and I will be with you always, even until the end of this age" (Matthew 28:16-20 and Mark 16:15-16).

One of the four Gospel accounts is the book of Luke. Luke was a physician who, although not an eye-witness of Jesus, became a follower who carefully studied everything about Jesus and His ministry and then arranged it chronologically to assure Theophilus that what he had been taught was true. Luke wrote a second letter to tell "the rest of the story" (as Paul Harvey used to say). We know it as the book of Acts. Acts continues where the Gospel of Luke leaves off. Here, Luke records the acts of the apostles in the first century and the beginning of Christ's church.

So let's dive further into this treasure trove of Scripture and see what this *discipleship* thing is all about....

The first chapter of Acts tells us that Judas (Iscariot) was replaced by a man named Matthias. In Acts chapter two, we learn that Jesus used Peter to establish His church. At the end of Peter's long sermon (at Pentecost), he "...warned them.... He begged them, 'Save yourselves from the evil of today's people!' Then those people who accepted what Peter said were baptized. About three thousand people were added to the number of believers that day. They spent their time learning the apostles' teaching, sharing, breaking bread, and praying together" (Acts 2:40-42). *Discipleship.*

Remember, many Jews had gathered in Jerusalem for "Pentecost," a Jewish holiday that took place fifty days after "Passover." With that in mind, you can better understand the reference to all the believers meeting together and "sharing everything." The locals were even selling their property and sharing with anyone who needed anything. "The believers met together in the Temple every day. They ate together in their homes, happy to share their food with joyful hearts. They praised God and were liked by all the people. Every day the *Lord added* those who were being saved to the group of believers" (Acts 2:44-47). [Note that *God* brought in those who believed and obeyed Him; they weren't voted in, so I'm sure personalities varied – a lot. Discipleship is **not** about you making *mini me's*; it's all about sharing *Jesus* and *His* Word.]

In Acts chapters three and four, we learn about Peter and John healing a man who was crippled and using the people's amazement as an opportunity to teach the Jews about Jesus. The Jewish leaders were upset and put Peter and John in jail so they could question them further the next day. "But many of those who had heard Peter and John preach believed the things they said. There were now about five thousand in the group of believers" (Acts 4:4). The next day, the Jewish Council questioned Peter and John and were amazed that although these men hadn't any formal education, they weren't afraid to speak; and "...they *realized* that they had been with Jesus" (Acts 4:13). That's what I want others to realize about me; I have been with Jesus.

----- That's the take-away. The *goal* of discipleship is to **reflect** Jesus.

The Jewish leaders knew they could not deny the miraculous healing; so after having Peter and John leave the meeting, the Council decided to warn them *not* to talk about Jesus anymore so that the news would not continue to spread. When the Jewish Council called Peter and John back into the meeting and gave their stern instructions, Peter and John told the Council they *had* to tell what they had seen and heard because that was what *God* wanted them to do. The leaders had no choice but to let them go, but they kept looking for ways to stop them. Peter and John went back and reported to the group of believers. They all praised God and asked that He help them share the message of His Word. God answered miraculously (Acts 4:16-31).

Acts chapter five exposes a couple who misrepresented a donation because they wanted to be *seen* as generous, but Peter says they were lying to *God*. Overall, the group of believers had a good reputation and kept growing. The apostles were miraculously healing the sick and casting out evil spirits; a group of Jewish leaders from the sect of the Sadducees became jealous and took *all* the apostles and put them in jail. This time, though, an angel miraculously led them out during the night and told them to keep preaching in the Temple, which they did.

When the leaders reconvened the next day, they sent men to get the apostles from the jail. The men reported back that everything was still closed and locked and the guards were still there, but the jail was *empty*. Somebody reported that the same men who'd been jailed were now *teaching* people in the Temple. The soldiers had to bring the apostles back without force because they were afraid of the people. When the leaders asked the apostles *why* they weren't following the strict orders they'd been given, "Peter and the other apostles answered, 'We must obey God, not human authority!'" (Acts 5:29).

The Jewish leaders were furious when Peter claimed – again - that **Jesus** was the one Whom God had sent to *save* His people and that *all* people could repent and have their sins forgiven. Gamaliel, a respected Jew from the sect of the Pharisees, warned these leaders that if this was a *false* movement, it would fizzle out as others had; but if it was from *God,* they could *not* stop it. He advised them to let these men go free; the other leaders followed Gamaliel's advice to let the apostles go free - but not before beating them and warning them to never speak in the name of Jesus again.

I love the attitude of the apostles as they were freed: "The apostles left the meeting full of joy because they were given the honor of suffering disgrace for Jesus. Every day in the Temple and in people's homes they continued teaching the people and telling the Good News – that Jesus is the Christ" (Acts 5:41-42).

Eventually, internal turmoil arose because the Greek-speaking followers said *their* widows weren't getting their share of the food that was given out every day. The twelve apostles did not want to detract from their call to spread the gospel; they had the whole group choose seven men "full of the Holy Spirit" to fill the physical need that had arisen (and to keep racism from distracting the church from its purpose). The church kept growing, and even several of the Jewish priests believed and obeyed (Acts Ch. 6).

Stephen was one of the seven chosen servants; he later became the first Christian martyr (Acts Ch. 7). From both Biblical and historical references, we learn that many of the apostles and other Christians, like Stephen, were martyred. Most of the believers were scattered because of persecution, leaving only the apostles in Jerusalem (Acts 8:1,3-4). In Acts chapter eight, we also learn about the work of Philip, another of the chosen seven servants. We're also told here about a Jew named Saul (from the Pharisee Sect), who was so zealous for what he believed that he persecuted Christians and *tried* to *destroy* the church, but "wherever they (Christians) were scattered, they told people the Good News."

Saul ended up being converted to Christianity (initially called "The Way") because of a miraculous intervention and calling by Jesus Himself (Acts Ch. 9). Right away, Saul started preaching in Damascus, where he had originally been going to get permission to arrest and kill more Christians. His proofs that Jesus is the Christ were so powerful, his own people made plans to kill him - plans thwarted when followers of Jesus helped Saul escape in a basket through the city wall.

Saul then tried to join a group of followers in Jerusalem, but they were afraid of him. They did not believe he was sincerely changed. Barnabas, the encourager, took Saul under his wing and told the apostles about how the Lord had spoken to Saul on the road to Damascus and then how Saul had preached there. Saul stayed with the followers in Jerusalem and preached until (for his protection from opposition) they sent him first to Caesarea and then to Tarsus. (Maybe, like Barnabas, *you* have the gift of encouragement? Even if you are not a brave, zealous speaker, you **can** be an encourager of one.)

Later, on one of his missionary journeys, Saul begins to be called Paul; he is also called an apostle of Jesus. As part of his God-given ministry, he ends up writing a number of letters to individuals and churches in the first century, many of which later would become part of our Bible - the inspired Word of God. (God used Saul/Paul with his zeal pointed in the right direction.)

The remainder of Acts chapter nine records healings that Peter did in Lydda and Joppa. Chapter ten recounts the vision of Cornelius (a Roman officer and also a believer in God) and the vision of Peter. These two visions helped Peter better understand that God did **not** send Jesus *only* for the Jews. "Peter began to speak: 'I really understand now that to God every person is the same. In every country God accepts *anyone* who worships Him and does what is right. You know the message that God has sent to the people of Israel is the Good News that peace has come through Jesus Christ. Jesus is the Lord of *all* people!'" (Acts 10:34-36).

Peter continued to preach the truth. The Jewish Christians who'd come with him were amazed to see the Holy Spirit poured out upon these new *Gentile* believers also – as had happened among their own people on the

"Day of Pentecost." "Peter said, 'Can anyone keep these people from being baptized with water? They have received the Holy Spirit just as we did!' So Peter ordered that they be baptized in the name of Jesus Christ. Then they asked Peter to stay with them for a few days" (Acts 10:47-48).

We learn from Acts chapter eleven that Peter had to *defend* his actions of going into a *Gentile* home and eating with them. But when the believers heard his testimony, they praised God because He was "...allowing other nations to *turn* to Him and *live*" (Acts11:18). This chapter also records the spread of the Good News – to both Jews and Gentiles - as followers of Christ were scattered during the persecution of new believers after Stephen's death. The church in Jerusalem sent Barnabas to check it out and make sure the new believers had been taught correctly. Barnabas was glad to see how God had blessed these people, and he encouraged them. Then he went to Tarsus to find Saul and brought him back to Antioch, where they both continued to meet with the church and teach people for a whole year. (I believe they were *discipling* others during this time.) "In Antioch the followers were called *Christians* for the first time" (Acts 11:26). Chapter eleven ends with a prophet telling about a severe famine coming; because of this, the believers there sent a voluntary donation to the elders in Judea through Barnabas and Saul. (Note again, these were **non**-Jews helping **Jews**.)

Herod Agrippa was treating people belonging to the church horribly and had even ordered James (John's brother) to be killed with a sword. When he saw that this made the Jewish leaders extremely happy, Herod arrested Peter and had him guarded by *sixteen* soldiers! Herod's *plan* was to hand Peter over to the Jews for execution after the Passover, but the church was fervently praying for Peter. God answered that prayer by sending an angel who miraculously led Peter out of jail and down the street before leaving Peter on his own. Peter suddenly realized that what had happened wasn't just a dream. He had been bound with chains and asleep between two soldiers, while other soldiers guarded the door. The chains had fallen off his hands; he'd dressed and followed the angel past two sets of guards; and then the iron gate leading out to the street had opened by itself! (Acts Ch. 12).

When Peter realized how God had saved him, he went to a home where believers were gathered together and praying. The servant girl was so excited to see him that she left him locked outside the door while she went to tell the group. They didn't believe her, but Peter continued knocking until they finally opened the door. Even though they had been praying for him, they were *shocked* to see him there. ---**Never forget this**: *God's Power is far greater than even our greatest faith.* ---

Peter told them everything that had happened and said, "Tell James and the other believers what happened" (Acts 12:17). This James is thought to be the half-brother of Jesus (credited with writing the New Testament book of James), since John's brother James had already been killed by this time. We can assume that James became a follower of Jesus sometime after Jesus' resurrection - maybe even at Pentecost – because we learned earlier that "...even Jesus' brothers did not believe in Him" (John 7:5).

King Herod died suddenly from an infestation of worms brought on because he refused to give God glory and instead accepted worship for himself from the people who proclaimed that his voice was like that of a god, not a human. Opposition to the church was destroyed for a time, and "God's message continued to spread and reach people" (Acts 12:24).

Paul and Barnabas were sent from the church at Antioch on a missionary journey, accompanied by John Mark, a young man who later abandoned them and went home before the journey was completed. After Paul and Barnabas returned to Antioch, some people came from Judea telling the non-Jewish believers they could *not* be saved if they were not circumcised (Old Testament Jewish Law). Paul and Barnabas argued strongly *against* this teaching; so the church in Antioch sent them and some others to the apostles and elders in Jerusalem to discuss the issue at hand. Peter reminded the church leaders that God had shown His acceptance of non-Jews and asked why they were trying to put a heavy load on *non*-Jews to obey the Old Law when even *they* couldn't do it. Peter stated, "But we believe that *we* and *they* too will be *saved* by the *grace* (free gift) of the Lord Jesus" (Acts 15:11).

After the issue was resolved, everyone listened to the testimonies of Paul and Barnabas about all the miracles and signs God had done through them among these non-Jewish believers. James brought up Peter's reminder of how God had shown His love for the non-Jewish people and then showed how the Old Testament prophecies *also* agreed that other nations would be accepted. The church leaders wrote a letter and sent witnesses to attest to the fact that non-Jews should *not* have to carry a heavy load, but advised, among other things avoiding food "...that has been offered to idols...and any kind of sexual sin. If you stay away from these things, you will do well. Good-bye" (Acts 15:29).

After some time, Judas and Silas returned to Jerusalem, while Paul and Barnabas stayed in Antioch and continued to preach the Good News. Eventually, Paul told Barnabas that they should go back through all the other towns where they had preached, checking on the new Christians and encouraging them. Barnabas wanted to take his cousin John Mark again, but Paul did not. This disagreement was so strong that Paul and Barnabas chose different traveling companions and went different directions. I think it is important to note here that they did *not* speak poorly of one another and held *no* animosity toward one another and that they still preached the *same* message. In fact, Barnabas must have done a great job of discipling John Mark because later in his life, Paul asks for John Mark, saying that he would be a help to him in his work. Paul later sends greetings from Mark and gives the church instructions to welcome him; Mark is also listed as one of Paul's fellow-workers. (II Timothy 4:11; Colossians 4:10-11; Philemon 1:24)

Most of the rest of the book of Acts talks about Paul's further missionary journeys, but I want to point out a few specific passages. Acts 16:1-5 describes the young man Timothy and how Paul desired to bring him along in his travels. Not only could Timothy help Paul, but Paul could also appease the Jewish side of Timothy's family while discipling him. Acts 16:22-34 describes an instance when Paul and Silas were unlawfully beaten with rods and then thrown into jail where they were put far inside the prison with their feet pinned down in stocks. "About midnight Paul and Silas were praying and singing songs to God as the other prisoners listened." But then all of the sudden there was a big earthquake; *all* the prisoners were *freed* when their chains fell off and the doors of the jail broke open. The jailer knew he would be held accountable and was about to kill himself with his sword, but he stopped when Paul shouted, "Don't hurt yourself! We are *all* here" (quoted: Acts 16:25,28).

We are *not* told *why* the other prisoners were in prison, but the example of Paul and Silas must have kept them from leaving! The jailer asked Paul and Silas what he must do to be saved, and they answered that he must believe in the Lord Jesus. "At that hour of the night the jailer took Paul and Silas and washed their wounds. Then he and all his people were baptized immediately. After this the jailer took Paul and Silas home and gave them food. He and his family were very happy because they now believed in God" (Acts 16:33-34).

So, we've seen how Jesus discipled others, especially the twelve. We've seen how the early Christians had fellowship together and spread the gospel through word and deed. We've seen how people like Saul, John Mark, and James (the half-brother of Jesus) were able to *change* because of the power of God. Now I'd like to look specifically at two young men: Timothy (whose mother and grandmother were Jewish, but whose father was a Gentile) and Titus (a Gentile believer). Although *not* physically related to either of these men, Paul called each of them his "*child* in the faith" and gave instructions on how to go about teaching and discipling others.

Paul says, "You then, Timothy, my child, be strong in the grace we have in Christ Jesus. You should teach people whom you can trust the things you and many others have heard me say. Then they will be able to teach others" (II Timothy 2:1-2). Both Timothy and Titus are encouraged to be good examples to the believers and to teach Scripture, *not* wasting their time with genealogies or arguments about words or anything else that would not be helpful, but to *focus* on Jesus and the Scriptures, relying on God's Spirit. - (And *that*, my friends, is discipleship in a nutshell.)

God wants *you* to be the change regarding racism and prejudice, and He has **empowered** you to do so. "I will pour out My Spirit on *all kinds* of people" (Joel 2:28). Remember, in chapter three of this book, we learned that if we want to make a difference, we must lean on the *Spirit's* power - *not* our own. The Old Testament prophet Zechariah reminds us of this when he shares God's message to the governor of Judah (Zerubbabel) and to himself, respectively:

"'You will **not** succeed by your own strength or by your own power, but by **My** Spirit,'

says the Lord All-Powerful....

'Zerubbabel has laid the foundation of this Temple, and he *will* complete it.'...

'The people should **not** think that *small* beginnings are unimportant'" (Zechariah 4:6,9,10).

Jesus told a parable which showed that His kingdom/church would start small, but would grow to minister to all those around: "The kingdom of heaven is like a mustard seed that a man planted in his field. That seed is the *smallest* seed of all seeds, but when it grows, it is one of the largest garden plants. It becomes big enough for the wild birds to come and build nests in its branches" (Matthew 13:31-32). Remember, Christ's church is made up of individual Christians; it is **not** a physical building.

God has done (and continues to do) His part. He loves us - *all of us* - so much that He became *one of us* (His own creation) and then died for us - *all of us* - to redeem us from our slavery to sin, making a way for us to have relationship with Him again. Jesus took away our sin (the barrier that kept us from Him) and replaced it with **His** Spirit. He offers this as a free gift – to *every one of us*.

The price? His life.   –   His offer? A gift

Will you accept His offer? It is my hope that you, too, will prayerfully *choose* peace, love, and unity and *act* on that choice by **investing** in your *own* relationship with God and ***discipling*** others to follow Jesus' example. ***He*** will change the world *through you*!

Remember - as the angel told Mary, regarding Elizabeth's pregnancy as well as her own (Luke 1:37):

"God can do anything!"

Final Thoughts to My Readers

*I never dreamed to become an author; I was merely given a dream, a story that I could **not** hold inside when I saw the world around me in such pain caused by racism and prejudice. It has become very clear to me – and I hope now to you too - that racism and prejudice are from the evil one. We cannot fight him with our own power, but we can with God's help. I have tried to give you a taste of what God desires and what He has to offer. I hope the insights and experiences I have shared in this book have created an appetite for more – more of God and His Word, for God is our Creator and truly has **all** the answers.*

What I want you to understand first and foremost is that God wants to have a personal relationship with you – to adopt you as His own child. He longs to give you the free gifts of salvation, the forgiveness of your sins, and the power of the indwelling Holy Spirit. He offers you His full protection, the fruit of the Spirit, and joy in relationships with others - even if they're different from you.

But the choice is still yours.

What does God want from you? He wants you to love Him and reflect His love to others. He has given you unique gifts to use. Will you accept His challenge to use them? The prophet Micah put it this way: "The Lord has told you, human, what is good; He has told you what He wants from you: to do what is right to other people, love being kind to others, and live humbly, obeying your God"

(Micah 6:8).

*My hope and prayer is that you will continue to grow in Christ – that you have **not** simply read another book, but that you will take the lessons learned from what I've shared and apply them to your own life. **Be** a disciple of Christ*

– and **disciple** others. Love others the way Christ loves you. Be the change. Stop racism and prejudice dead in their tracks.

Love always,

Debbie Potter

About the Author

Debbie Potter wants to give you the gifts of love, light, and life in a world full of defiance, darkness, and death. She is especially passionate about the perfect peace, unity, and love God offers, and which is so desperately needed during this time of rampant racism and hatred. Although she spent her childhood and most of her adult married life in smaller towns, Debbie lived as a single woman in Portland, Oregon while attending a small Christian college and later lived and worked for a few years in Seattle, Washington (known at the time as "the melting pot of the world"). It broke her heart to see these two lovely cities from her past broken and devastated by the 2020 Black Lives Matter Riots, and she knew the time had come for her to write <u>Ebony & Ivory: Promoting Peace, Love, and Unity in a Racist World</u>.

Debbie draws from the Bible and her education, trainings, and experiences during her six decades of life in the USA. She was happily married to minister Dewey Potter just shy of thirty-four years before becoming a widow. She gained insights from that relationship as well as from others. An especially vivid dream she had years ago, prompted by principles taught in the Biblical book of Ephesians, has also guided her life and the content of this book.

Debbie currently lives in Northern California. She enjoys spending time with her huge beloved dog Bear, helping older people, caring for babies and other young children, reading, singing, and generally enjoying the people and animals in her life - and the beauty in nature.

www.ingramcontent.com/pod-product-compliance
Lightning Source LLC
Chambersburg PA
CBHW060501280326
41933CB00014B/2817